JOY IN COORG

Tilak Ponappa has a PhD from The Ohio State University, USA, where he conducted research in the areas of plant biochemistry and molecular biology. He moved to Coorg several years ago to manage the family coffee plantation. He currently lives there with assorted dogs, cats and wildlife.

JOY IN COORG

TILAK PONAPPA

RUPA

Published by
Rupa Publications India Pvt. Ltd 2019
7/16, Ansari Road, Daryaganj
New Delhi 110002

Sales centres:
Allahabad Bengaluru Chennai
Hyderabad Jaipur Kathmandu
Kolkata Mumbai

ISBN: 978-93-5333-317-1

First impression 2019

10 9 8 7 6 5 4 3 2 1

The moral right of the author has been asserted.

Printed at Nutech Print Services, Faridabad

To Bojie and Ponnu

Contents

Introduction

Joy in Coorg is set in the little district of Coorg (Kodagu) in Karnataka and takes a humorous look at the life of Joyappa (Joy, for short). Coorg is a beautiful area that is predominantly rural in nature with the economy being driven by its agricultural produce—primarily coffee and pepper. The densely forested, hilly region is nestled in the Western Ghats and is home to a wide array of plants and wildlife. Sport, primarily hockey, plays a major role in the lives of the people of the district, many of whom have represented the nation internationally. Over the years, a career in the armed forces has become a much-respected career option, with several residents having served the country with great distinction and honour.

Joyappa lives on a coffee estate with his wife, Susheela, the daughter of a war hero. Susheela is socially responsible, fashion conscious, and generally far better organized than her husband. Joyappa was a star hockey player in his youth, before injury curtailed a promising career. He now runs his coffee estate, but not as efficiently as Susheela would like. Joyappa enjoys his food and drink and likes to spend time with his somewhat irresponsible college friends, Chomu and Charlie, neither of whom meets with Susheela's approval. The stories touch upon Joyappa's attempts to have a good time despite Susheela's best efforts to get him to be careful with his diet, drinking and other activities.

During the course of his adventures Joyappa has to negotiate various hazards including his in-laws, Susheela's friends, hikes through the wilderness, wild animals and highway robbers. Through all of these events, Joyappa's greatest challenge is to stay on the right side of his wife.

1

Joyappa's Day Out

I

Joyappa's slumber ended abruptly. The two cats, Tiny and Bug, having kept him warm through the chilly night, decided that he needed to be woken up. Bug pulled aside the curtains to let the morning sunlight hit him directly in the face. Joyappa groaned and turned away, hoping for another half hour of sleep. He should have known better. Tiny launched herself from the nearby window sill and using Joyappa's protuberant belly as a springboard, took off like a rocket and landed on a nearby bookshelf. Half a dozen of his wife's self-help books crashed to the floor.

Joyappa cursed, but not too loudly. His propensity for swearing was considered low-class by his wife and he did not want to get her started so early in the day.

His head felt heavy and his tongue swollen. 'That's what cheap brandy and cheaper rum will do to a fellow,' he mumbled to himself, before rolling out of bed. His wife, Susheela, had probably been up and about for hours, as her side of the bed was cold.

Joyappa picked the books off the ground, then dropped some dry food into the cats' dishes and watched them eat noisily. His morning ablutions were performed quickly and not very hygienically. Joyappa put on his favourite jeans and a loose tee-shirt that he hoped would conceal his paunch. After all, he didn't want to get his wife worked up about his appearance either.

Susheela was on the telephone with her best friend. She looked up at Joyappa and pointed to his place at the dining table. He cringed. Today's breakfast would be similar to yesterday's, which had been similar to that of the day before. In fact, today's breakfast was almost identical to every breakfast that his wife had served him since the doctor had said that his cholesterol levels were too high. There was oat porridge, a slice of whole-wheat toast, homemade marmalade and black tea. Joyappa cringed because what he really longed for was a generous helping of *pandi* curry and crisp *akki otti*. At the thought of the wonderful pork concoction, with chunks of fat floating in the dark, oily gravy, Joyappa smiled, and it was all he could do to keep from salivating. Then he looked at the bland, supposedly healthy fare in front of him and his smile faded.

Joyappa finished the last of his lukewarm, slightly congealed porridge. As he chewed half-heartedly on a piece of toast, he looked at his wife. Susheela was pretty, and she knew it. Her once wavy hair was now straight and appeared to have red and light brown highlights. Despite the early hour, her skin looked flawless. Joyappa, largely ignorant of the magic of modern cosmetics, marveled at his wife's youthful appearance. After two children, she still had the figure of a teenager. Perhaps it was the years of high-impact aerobics, followed by her present fitness regime of yoga and Pilates, that kept her svelte. Perhaps it was eating less than a self-respecting bird. Or perhaps it was all of the above. Whatever the reason, he felt a twinge of resentment when he looked down at his own bulging belly.

Joyappa took a sip of tepid tea and wished it was strong filter coffee. But his wife had read something in one of her obscure health magazines that extolled the virtues of tea. Idly, he wondered, if one was unwilling to drink coffee, wasn't it hypocritical to grow it? But he didn't dare voice his concerns.

Timmy came into the dining room, and seated himself opposite his father without a greeting. The boy was home on vacation from his school in the Nilgiri Hills, while his older sister spent her holidays in Bangalore at an aunt's place. Seeing Timmy, Susheela quickly terminated her phone call and smiled at the boy. Mother and son proceeded to exchange 'Good mornings'. Then they began to exchange kisses over and over again.

Joyappa almost gagged. He'd grown up in an undemonstrative household, so he hoped that his son wouldn't get soft-headed with all that motherly love. Timmy was undoubtedly a mama's boy. For a fleeting moment, Joyappa had expected boarding school to toughen up the kid. But after observing his wife's actions, all of his hopes on that score were dashed. He realized that if Rambo had been faced with this sort of an upbringing, he would probably have been an author of romantic novels instead of a one-man army.

Joyappa silently watched Susheela bring their son a plate of crisp bacon and scrambled eggs from the kitchen. She sat down beside Timmy and proceeded to lovingly fork the food into the boy's mouth. Joyappa was torn between a deep craving for the forbidden bacon and eggs, and a horrified fascination as he watched someone perfectly capable of feeding himself, being hand-fed instead.

Timmy, aided by his mother, soon polished off his meal and left to do what he liked best: play computer games. Although Joyappa had tried to get his son to play hockey and other outdoor sports, the boy had exhibited neither the interest nor the requisite physical coordination. Joyappa had been a star of his school and college hockey teams before a knee injury put an end to his career. As he had had some memorable moments both on and off the hockey field, he was disappointed at his son's lack of enthusiasm for the sport. Sometimes Joyappa wondered if Susheela considered the sport a bit lowbrow, and had thus dissuaded Timmy from playing.

Susheela cleared the table with her customary efficiency before addressing Joyappa. 'I'm spending the day at Ash's place, Joy,' she said. 'I'll take Timmy with me. I guess we should be back at six or so this evening.'

Not for the first time, Joyappa wondered why perfectly good names had to be shortened and anglicized by Susheela. The 'Ash' in question, was Asha, Susheela's friend from the exclusive boarding school where they had spent their formative years. Asha, in turn, referred to Susheela as 'Sue'. In fact, Joyappa wasn't exactly thrilled that Timmy's name had been shortened from Thimmaiah, but his protests had been brushed aside by Susheela.

Susheela proceeded to give Joyappa instructions for the day, 'You had better head over to the Forest Block, and supervise the weeding. You know how expensive labour is these days, so it would be best if you spent the day there.'

'Sure, dear,' said Joyappa meekly, as his mind went into overdrive trying to get out of supervision—the most boring activity he could imagine. The area Susheela referred to was located about ten kilometres from their house. The saving grace, as far as he was concerned, was the lack of cell phone coverage in the area, which meant that Susheela could not check on him.

'Here's a list, along with a thousand rupees' continued Susheela, 'we will need some groceries from town on your way back from the estate. Now you'd better hurry and get ready.'

'I *am* ready,' mumbled Joyappa. Susheela cleared her throat and looked meaningfully at his chest. Joyappa glanced down, and sure enough, his tee-shirt was smeared with marmalade and bread crumbs. He hurriedly changed into a clean shirt, which unfortunately accentuated his paunch, and returned to the dining room.

Susheela handed him his lunch box before leaving the room with a toss of her fashionably styled hair. Without bothering to look, Joyappa knew that it would contain two low-fat cheese sandwiches on wholewheat bread, and a banana. How, he wondered, was a fully grown, red-blooded male expected to survive on this boring, bland stuff! No grease, no spice, no flavour, no damn fun. Joyappa kept his face impassive, but almost wept on the inside.

Joyappa hopped into his trusty old jeep, and drove slowly along the potholed road leading to the estate. The scenery, typical of Coorg, was beautiful, with mist-wreathed peaks flanking lush wetlands. But Joyappa couldn't quite appreciate his surroundings; his head hurt and the craving for nicotine was making him grumpier by the minute. By the time he drove the last kilometre up a bumpy mud road, his mood had turned foul.

Joyappa stopped at the traditional bamboo gate or *ubba* and decided that he didn't want to get down and open it himself. He honked a couple of times hoping one of his workers would open the gate. As there was no response, he banged down on the horn—yet no one appeared. Furious, he sounded the horn for a whole minute. A couple of startled doves flew away, but there was still no one to open the gate. His anger escalated and he pushed violently on the horn for three more minutes. In the nearby jungle, a mongoose, which had been poised to pounce on a spectacled cobra, decided to leave abruptly. Unable to hear the racket, the puzzled snake gratefully slithered off to safety. Normally noisy woodpeckers fell silent and took off for quieter surroundings.

Still no one appeared. Joyappa was furious. Usually calm on the surface in his wife's presence, he was now absolutely livid. He began to swear. The word 'creative' may never have been used to describe Joyappa by his nearest or dearest, but anyone within earshot of him now would have argued that the man possessed a certain flair with words. Just that the words were not particularly nice ones. He seemed to touch upon every topic forbidden in polite conversation: there were serious questions raised about people's maternity, paternity, intelligence and dietary preferences. These were interspersed with references to bodily functions and body parts. It was a swearing master class—delivered with great fluency, at a high decibel level and in several different languages. Joyappa's explosion over a seemingly trivial matter could be attributed to his feeling of being half-starved, hungover, and deprived of nicotine and caffeine.

Finally, Joyappa freed his paunch from under the steering wheel and got out of the vehicle. He walked over to the gate and violently pulled out the bamboo barrier. Then he forced himself back in the jeep and drove through the open gate.

Joyappa struggled out of the vehicle and proceeded to close the gate. As he replaced the last of the bamboo poles, a twig cracked behind him. He turned around to see the smiling face of his supervisor.

'Namaste, sir,' said the young man, as he made an odd movement with his head that was a combination between a nod and a shake.

'Where were you, Ashok? I've been trying to get someone to open the damn gate for half an hour,' he growled.

'My name's Babu, sir,' said the supervisor, again with that obsequious bobble of his head.

'Whatever, you little…' Joyappa stopped himself just in time. He remembered that it was Susheela who had hired the fellow, and he didn't want to be responsible for losing yet another supervisor.

'I'm sorry, sir. I heard your horn and came running from the opposite end of the estate as soon as I could.'

Joyappa glowered at Babu. In his fevered, unhappy state, he perceived that the supervisor had a sly look on his face. In fact, the fellow didn't look like he had been running at all. Could the little twit have waited behind a tree just to torture him? Suspicious though he was, Joyappa felt that he could not chastise the man without any proof. So he just stared at him for a while, unsure about what to do. Babu's sunny disposition had long since vanished and his knees began to wobble under the hostile scrutiny.

Presently, Joyappa spotted a bulge in Babu's shirt pocket. His face cleared.

'You got any beedis?' he asked.

'I don't smoke, sir.' squeaked Babu.

'Don't lie to me,' thundered Joyappa. 'What's that in your pocket? Have you sprouted a single breast since I saw you last?'

Babu fished out a packet of beedies and a matchbox from his pocket. 'They're not mine, sir. I bought them for a friend.'

Joyappa almost smiled when he saw the beedies. 'Well, tell your friend that I'm borrowing a couple,' he said.

Joyappa lit up and inhaled deeply. His mood was immediately transformed as the nicotine soothed his nerves.

'How's work going?'

'All of the workers are present, sir. We're making good progress,' said Babu, with a tentative smile.

'Hmph, let's go take a look at the work. I will follow you,' said Joyappa, visibly more relaxed.

Babu turned and headed off briskly down a little footpath. Hundreds of spiders had spun elaborate webs between the rows of coffee bushes. The supervisor must not have been more than five feet two inches tall, and Joyappa towered above him. Fortunately for Babu, almost all of the webs appeared to be constructed several inches above his head. However, as Joyappa followed the shorter man, he was subjected to that most uncomfortable feeling of having spider webs wrapped around his hair, eyes and mouth. The sensation was ticklish and distinctly unpleasant. His nerves, hitherto calmed by Babu's beedi, began to jangle again.

As Joyappa's blood pressure began to mount, his cell phone buzzed, indicating that he had a message. Taken aback, since there typically was no mobile phone coverage in the area, he stopped abruptly. As he extricated the phone from his too-tight jeans, Joyappa ducked to avoid a particularly large web across the path. In the process, he put his head in the middle of an ant nest on a nearby bush. The nest was skillfully constructed from coffee leaves and inhabited by thousands of red ants. They reacted predictably. They descended in large numbers upon the foreign object. Some of the ants remained on Joyappa's head, while others decided to wage war on his face, neck and torso below.

'Nghyaaaa,' screamed Joyappa, as the angry insects began to bite whatever flesh they came in contact with. In fact, they didn't just bite his flesh and retire. They bit and hung on for dear life, all the while secreting some foul smelling liquid. Poor Joyappa was in incredible pain.

At the odd sound made by his boss, Babu turned around. He saw that Joyappa had flung his cell phone down and was vigorously rubbing his head. He was also making further peculiar sounds that Babu couldn't quite decipher. Then Joyappa pulled off his shirt revealing a frighteningly thick mat of black hair covering his chest and back, dotted with rapidly moving reddish-orange spots. He began to frantically remove the ants from his body, all the while hopping and grunting in pain.

Babu watched the drama helplessly. He wanted to help, but didn't dare touch the hirsute body in front of him. Finally, after much swearing and moaning, Joyappa got rid of the last of the ants. Babu couldn't help but notice that his employer's hair (on both head and body) now defied gravity and stood at various odd angles.

Babu picked up the cell phone that had landed on a pile of

dead leaves. Joyappa pulled on his shirt and grabbed the proffered phone. Through some quirk of fate, his friend Chomu had managed to text him. Chomu wanted to meet at the bottom of the hill in about fifteen minutes to discuss an important matter.

Joyappa made a split-second decision. He felt that his pal's summons should take precedence over work on the estate, and his managerial duties could be carried out by intimidation.

Fixing Babu with a piercing glare, he growled, 'I want this entire block weeded, and it had better be a pucca job. Do you understand? Is that clear, Harish?'

'Yes, sir,' said Babu, concluding sadly that his boss would never get his name right.

'I've got to see to some urgent work, but I'll be back soon,' lied Joyappa. 'Now open the gate for me and close it after I leave.'

II

Thanks to his friend's message, Joyappa felt as if the large black cloud hovering over him all morning had been blown away. Suddenly, he noticed the fragrance of wild jasmine that grew in between the *Duranta* hedge lining the estate. The harsh laughter of the hornbills seemed like sweet music to him. He took a few seconds to admire the brilliant blue of a kingfisher, and even spent a couple of minutes observing an intricate spider web spanning the lower branches of a red cedar sapling. His nerves, which so recently were on edge at the prospect of having to supervise weeding, had been calmed.

Joyappa turned off the cell phone so that Susheela would not be able to check on his whereabouts, hopped into the old jeep and sped down the hill. From some recess of his memory he summoned up a quote and began to shout at the top of his lungs, 'Free at *last*! Free at *last*! Thank God almighty, free at *last*!' He spent the next couple of minutes trying to figure out who he was quoting. Definitely a great person, but who *was* it? He was sure it was Luther someone. Was it Martin Luther or Lex Luthor? Maybe it was Martin Luther King, Jr. No, he concluded quite incorrectly, it was probably someone called Luther Vandross.

By then, Joyappa was close to the large wild fig tree where he was supposed to meet Chomu. He dodged a gigantic pothole, stopped under the tree and lit up the second 'borrowed' beedi as he waited for his friend.

A few minutes later, a rusty off-white pick-up truck pulled up just behind the jeep. Two contrasting figures stepped out and headed towards Joyappa. Chomu was short and stocky. He had light brown eyes and a prominent lower jaw that jutted forward giving him an aggressive appearance. Charlie, whose presence came as a pleasant surprise to Joyappa, was tall and thin, with a receding chin and greasy black hair styled in a 'mullet' that had been popular decades ago. Although he had never actually stated it, Joyappa had always felt that Charlie resembled some sort of aquatic bird. Not being particularly well-versed in bird nomenclature, he thought it might be a stork. On second thoughts, maybe he meant a crane; or possibly an egret—but *definitely* not a swan.

'Hi, Joya. Where you been, man?' said Chomu.

'Yeah Joya, long time, man,' said Charlie.

Joyappa was genuinely happy to see his friends. He high-fived his pals, and hugged them. Then, slightly embarrassed to show so much emotion, he punched their arms.

The three friends had known each other for years. Chomu and Joyappa were *chaddi*-buddies, having been friends since primary school, and roommates in college. While in college in Bangalore, Charlie had been assigned to their room in the hostel, and they had all instantly hit it off. The three friends had played hockey for their college, and as is often the case, the trials and tribulations of a team sport cemented their friendship.

Joyappa was the centre forward and had possessed many of the attributes required for the position. Some centre forwards scored goals by subtle means involving deception, body-feints, fancy stick work and anticipation. Joyappa most certainly did not belong to this breed. He was blessed with great speed and thick thighs that allowed him to accelerate and change direction rapidly. He was also fearless. The newspapers often described him as 'dashing'. And dash he did. In his insatiable desire to score goals, he had dashed into defenders, his own players, referees, and on one memorable occasion, even a goal post. His methods may have been crude, but they were undoubtedly effective. Having led his team to victory in the prestigious inter-collegiate tournament two years running, Joyappa had been earmarked for greater things. Unfortunately, in a crucial match during his final year in college, a wild sprint ended in a collision with the scorer's table. The resulting injury to his knee put a premature end to his sporting career.

Chomu lived alone in a large bungalow. His wife lived in Bangalore, ostensibly to educate their two girls in some fancy school. However, local gossips believed that the long-suffering woman moved to the city to avoid the temptation of clubbing her annoying husband over his thick head.

Charlie had never been married. His friends weren't quite

sure if it was by choice or necessity. He lived with his mother—a formidable woman who ran the family coffee estate with an iron hand, and still gave her only son a strict weekly allowance.

Joyappa wished he could meet his friends more frequently. When he was single, his pals had dropped in almost every day. Typically, these visits were extended drinking sessions, punctuated by the kind of antics and humour that can only be described as juvenile. After he married Susheela, the frequency of their visits gradually declined to the point where they had stopped altogether. The three buddies could hardly be called sensitive. Yet, the tacit disapproval that emanated from Susheela, like a cold-front from the Arctic, soon put an end to their regular meetings.

III

After the brief exchange of pleasantries, Joyappa was brought up to speed on the 'important matter' to which Chomu had alluded in his text message. It had been a long and oppressive monsoon season and Charlie wanted an outing. He'd lied to his mother, Gangavva, saying that the transmission of his pick-up truck required a tune-up. In reality, the vehicle was just fine, and although he wasn't sure about the purpose of a transmission, Charlie *was* sure that Mummy knew even less than he did about automobiles.

A quick plan was hatched without much thought about the consequences. The two vehicles were driven into town and Charlie's pick-up was parked in a crude enclosure sporting a garish yellow board with the legend, 'Warkshop—Car, Jeep, Auto, Tiller Repare.' The owner of the business, Velu, was even less mechanically inclined than Charlie. Consequently, no local resident dared to have his vehicle repaired at the workshop. These days, Velu's only business came from unsuspecting motorists passing through town.

Charlie, after sternly warning Velu not to touch the vehicle at any cost, tipped the mechanic for his trouble. The three friends, light of heart and with a song on their lips, piled into Joyappa's jeep and headed off to the bright lights of Mysore.

The travellers were enveloped in a warm glow as they reveled in their camaraderie.

Joyappa drove slowly, singing familiar songs with great enthusiasm. The songs in question had no redeeming features; they may have rhymed, but were performed loudly and tunelessly, and referred to issues that were decidedly vulgar.

As the jeep passed through the jungle, weaving between potholes, a herd of spotted deer scattered in fear. A quarter of an hour later, the buddies were still singing at the top of their voices. A panther, confused by the cacophony, abandoned the hard-earned kill that she had carried up a tree, and slipped deep into the jungle.

By the time they reached Hunsur, the three friends had sung themselves hoarse. Joyappa stopped at a roadside eatery and whispered an order for *kesari bath* (with extra ghee) and strong filter coffee (with extra sugar). The waiter, often used to rude tourists, was impressed at how polite these customers were and wished that everyone was as soft-spoken.

Duly fortified, the intrepid travellers proceeded to Mysore, communicating only in whispers. They decided that the first order of business would be to watch a movie. Charlie was assigned the task of choosing the film, and after careful examination of the garish posters plastered everywhere, directed

Joyappa to a dilapidated theatre in a shabby neighbourhood.

Charlie's choice was an action movie. The theatre was packed, so the only available seats were all the way in front. Chomu was in charge of procuring refreshments. He stocked up on stale popcorn, greasy chips, chocolate and soft drinks. Looking around, Charlie did not spot a single woman—which should have been fair warning about the impending show.

The lights dimmed and the movie started. If there was a plot, it was not a complicated one. There were car chases, improbable martial arts scenes featuring gravity-defying stunts, shoot-outs with automatic weapons, knife-wielding bad guys, and beautiful women with incredible bodies.

The audience cheered each victory of the leading man. Amazingly, the star emerged from each vigorous encounter (either romantic or violent) with every slicked-down hair in place, and with nary a scratch on his person. The audience loved it all. No one loved it more than Joyappa who, over the past several weeks, had been compelled by Susheela to watch a series of romantic comedies that bored him to tears.

The movie ended predictably. Most of the bad guys had been pummelled, shot, eviscerated, impaled or thrown off cliffs. The leader of the crooks and his right-hand man had managed a narrow escape that would no doubt lead to a sequel. Finally, the indomitable hero winked at the camera and began to get cosy with a well-endowed starlet who had no apparent inhibitions. As the credits began to roll, Joyappa and his buddies left their seats reluctantly, each of them hoping that Part VII of the series would be released without too much delay.

They stepped out into the street and before their eyes could adapt to daylight, Chomu almost fell into an open drain, while

Charlie had to jump to avoid a brown, gooey mound of dubious origin. With practiced ease, Joyappa and Chomu slipped on their very dark aviator sunglasses, while Charlie sported a similarly shaped pair of mirrored shades.

'Want to walk up the road before lunch?' asked Charlie.

'Okey-dokey,' replied Chomu out of the side of his mouth, mimicking the hero of the movie.

Charlie led the way, heading to an area frequented by students of a nearby women's college. As the three friends sauntered up the street, most of the young women discreetly crossed over to the other side. And could they be faulted? Because, heading towards them were three middle-aged men with thick, bristly moustaches, wearing tight blue jeans and sporting practically opaque sunglasses. This was the sort of danger their parents and grandparents had probably warned them about before they left home.

One unfortunate young woman was so engrossed in texting that she walked straight towards Charlie. Sensing a hazard, she suddenly looked up. Charlie smiled charmingly, revealing teeth stained by years of tobacco use, and winked. Fortunately, his eyes were invisible behind the mirrored shades. Yet, the overall effect of the encounter on the innocent young thing was remarkable. She executed a vertical leap of about 18 inches, before turning around and scurrying back the way she came. Charlie and his pals shrugged and looked mystified.

After admiring the scenery for a while, it was time for lunch. Joyappa was assigned the task of choosing a restaurant. When he dined out with Susheela, Joyappa was restricted to eating in impossibly expensive places that served insipid soups, salads and sandwiches. There were also occasions when he was forced to eat in the uppity clubs that Susheela had insisted they join. This was not to be one of those times.

Joyappa led his friends down a narrow alley. They had to step over sleeping dogs, dodge past cattle foraging through piles of rubbish, and avoid the ubiquitous autorickshaws, scooters and mopeds before they reached their destination. This was not the kind of establishment that Susheela would be caught dead in. Chomu and Charlie, however, gave Joyappa approving nods before they entered.

The restaurant was named, 'Chikkun Mattun Pork Canteen'. Whereas the name was not particularly creative, the rusty sign certainly got the message across. The newest customers of CMP Canteen chose a formica-topped table all the way in the back of the crowded dining area, just outside the kitchen. A pimply faced youth was summoned and asked to purchase several bottles of beer from a nearby liquor store.

After the beer arrived, what ensued could well be described as a carnivorous orgy. Although not completely neglected, the plant kingdom was poorly represented in the feast. A brief warm-up featuring chicken 'lollipops' and wings was followed by brain cutlets and fried pieces of sheep liver, kidneys and sweetbread. The main dish consisted of white rice smothered with pork curry. The pork was just the way Joyappa liked: meat on the bone and laden with fat. After months of deprivation, his body craved animal protein and lipids. He chomped, gnawed, slurped and crunched his way through the meal. A couple of the waiters watched the display, their lower jaws slack with amazement.

Finally sated, the three friends drained their beers and leaned back in their chairs. Chomu and Joyappa unbuttoned their jeans to accommodate their enlarged bellies. Charlie, who had also consumed a vast amount of food, exhibited no such concern. Looking at the bony, elongated figure next to him, Joyappa wondered, not for the first time, if his friend harboured pythons in his stomach.

The paan seller outside provided the final course. He laid out several betel leaves and filled them with pastes and powders of varied colour and consistency, before masterfully wrapping them up for his audience.

With their lips and teeth stained red and mouths too full to talk, the three buddies began to wander back to the jeep. While scratching his belly, Joyappa happened to look at his watch and nearly suffered cardiac arrest. *Susheela would be home in just one hour!*

Gesturing wildly, he pointed at his watch. Such was the understanding between the former team-mates that no words needed to be said. Charlie, who had not drunk as much beer as the others, quickly folded himself into the driver's seat, with Chomu next to him. Joyappa hopped into the back, looking more and more anxious with each passing minute. Charlie gunned the engine and took off. Fortunately, traffic was light and they made it out of town easily. Chomu and Joyappa dozed off about ten minutes into the journey.

Charlie drove rapidly, but was forced to stop near Hunsur thanks to the beer he had consumed at lunch. His passengers awoke with a start and joined him along the side of the road. Joyappa shook off his sleep amongst other things, looked at his watch and screamed, '*Ayyo! Pochi ra,*' which, roughly translated, meant that his goose was cooked.

Joyappa now took the wheel and blasted off. Hunsur passed

in a blur. Most of the rules of the Motor Vehicles Act were violated with impunity as dogs scooted aside, pedestrians dived for safety, two-wheelers ended up in ditches and even buses and enormous timber lorries were forced to yield to the speeding jeep. Chomu closed his eyes and hoped for the best, while Charlie's occasional screams were drowned out by either the blaring horn or the rattle of the abused vehicle's suspension.

The jeep came to a screeching halt in the little town of Panchavalli. Joyappa jumped out without explanation and limped (since his old injury was bothering him again) towards a nearby shop. In a couple of minutes, he returned with several bulging plastic bags filled with groceries, before his quest to break the land-speed record resumed.

The road had deteriorated to the point where there were more potholes than tarmac. Yet, Joyappa continued in the same vein. He dodged past the numerous vehicles ferrying workers back to their homes after a hard day's labour in the coffee plantations. Fortunately for everyone concerned, no wildlife crossed the road as the jeep sped through the forest and under the open check-post. Joyappa slowed down briefly to feed some monkeys with the lunch Susheela had packed that morning, before flooring the accelerator again.

With seven minutes remaining, Joyappa unloaded his passengers outside the workshop and proceeded. Chomu waved as he yelled, 'Good luck, Joya. Hurry!' while Charlie extended a long, skinny digit that Joyappa assumed was meant to be a thumbs-up.

Joyappa roared up the driveway. Relieved to see that Susheela was not back yet, he grabbed his purchases and limped into the house. With only a minute to go, he switched on the TV. A serious young woman was speaking about serious things that he couldn't quite understand. Quickly, he entered the bathroom, gargled with mouthwash and sprayed himself with an aerosol can lying nearby. He had intended to disguise the smells of tobacco, beer, paan and forbidden food with air-freshener, but in his haste, Joyappa had mistakenly sprayed himself with cockroach-killer, and was consequently wracked by a violent bout of coughing.

Joyappa quickly stretched out on the couch and covered himself with a blanket. Punctual as ever, Susheela parked outside at exactly six o'clock. She entered the house, followed by Timmy, who charged upstairs to his beloved laptop.

'Hello, dear,' said Susheela.

She was greeted by a dry, hacking cough from the couch. Concerned, she rushed over to her pale and tired-looking husband.

'Oh my gosh! Are you all right, Joy?' asked Susheela.

All Joyappa could do was cough and look at his wife pitifully. He was still perspiring from the high-speed drive and his heart continued to pound wildly.

She touched his forehead, which was unnaturally warm from the hectic activity, and said, 'Poor dear. You seem to be running a fever. You must have had a hard day on the estate.'

Susheela switched the TV to her husband's favourite sports channel and kissed him on the cheek. Overwhelmed by the complex mixture of odours that he gave off, she almost choked, but didn't utter a word out of consideration for the invalid.

'I don't want you exerting, dear. You had better rest tomorrow, as well. I'll get you something to drink,' said Susheela over her shoulder, as she headed off to the kitchen.

'Thanks, Susheela,' croaked Joyappa, as he settled down to watch two gigantic men in tiny, brightly coloured shorts pummelling each other in a wrestling ring. He idly wondered why no one ever seemed to get seriously hurt despite all the violence.

Tiny and Bug, spotting a warm place, jumped onto Joyappa's chest. He scratched Bug under the chin and Tiny behind her ears and both cats began to purr.

'Something very odd happened today,' said Susheela as she returned with a cup of tea and toast (wholewheat, of course). Her brow was furrowed in thought.

'My friend Jo called. You remember Jyoti, my classmate from college? She said that she saw you in Mysore today. I told her you were on the estate, but she swore you were strutting down the street with a couple of rough looking characters.'

Joyappa's heart skipped a beat. He was glad that Tiny's bushy tail now covered his face and masked the patently guilty look on it. Rather than answer, he burst into a loud, terrible coughing fit.

'Oh, you poor thing,' said Susheela with concern. 'It must have been someone else. Jo's eyesight was never very good.'

Joyappa coughed again, even more violently. His wife rushed off to look for some cough syrup, although the cats remained unperturbed. Joyappa covered his face with the blanket and smiled slyly. What an *amazing* day, he thought.

2

Joyappa Scores

I

Susheela had left early in the morning to meet some friends. The children were away and the estate workers had taken the day off for some reason. Joyappa was bored. He picked up a local newspaper and began to read random advertisements and stories. He tried to read the editorial and lost interest after the first couple of sentences. An advertisement extolling the haemorrhoid-shrinking and itch-reducing properties of an ointment caught his attention briefly.

He yawned noisily. Just as he was about to toss aside the newspaper, he happened to read that his family team was scheduled to play a hockey match that afternoon. He had been told about the match almost a month ago, but it had completely slipped his mind.

The hockey tournament was a big event in Coorg. For years, the small, land-locked area had produced brave warriors for the army, and outstanding hockey players for the state and country. Several years ago, a hockey tournament had been instituted, pitting the various clans (or families) against each other. The first tournament was a grand success and the event had grown from year to year so that hundreds of clans participated and thousands of spectators enjoyed the matches. Players located in different parts of the country made it a priority to represent their clans. Many of them travelled great distances at substantial personal cost to participate in the great hockey festival. In general, the tournament prompted much bonding and goodwill. Many heartwarming stories were heard about how feuding family members mended fences (or literally took them down, in some cases) after playing together on their teams. Conversely, quarrels sometimes arose over missed penalty strokes or poor defensive play. Fortunately, *these* minor disputes were not of the long-standing variety and were soon forgotten.

Some of the bigger families had many professional and semi-professional players and took themselves very seriously. There were other clans that struggled every year to find enough players to field a team. Joyappa's family belonged to the latter category.

This year, his family had decided to participate for only the second time since the inception of the tournament. The team was admittedly not one of the better ones, as only a couple of young men in their twenties had much playing experience. Joyappa had been asked to lead the team by the family elders, but his wife had absolutely forbidden him to play after receiving the results of his latest medical examination. Susheela's decision was a rational one, considering that Joyappa's blood pressure and cholesterol levels were dangerously high. Also, his knee probably needed to be replaced. Consequently, it was with a heavy heart that Joyappa had had to turn down the honour of captaining the team. *However*, he thought to himself, *there really should be no objection to my cheering on and supporting the team this afternoon*. So he called his friend, Chomu, who readily agreed to accompany him to the match.

II

Chomu picked up Joyappa in his shiny new car. Both men were attired in tight-fitting blue jeans and white tee-shirts.

Chomu pushed his dark glasses up and said, 'Hey, Joya. What's new?'

'Chommms,' yelled Joyappa, happily. 'What's happening, man?'

'Not much. Charlie's attending a wedding out of town, or we could have taken him along.'

'Yeah. Too bad. Would've been fun.'

Chomu drove his new car very fast. As usual, he was quite talkative. He took his eyes off the road often and looked at Joyappa, especially when he was emphasizing a point. Joyappa felt a little nervous when Chomu was driving, since he was constantly emphasizing some point or the other. Chomu's wife had been in Bangalore for a while now, and according to local gossip, didn't intend to come back and live with her husband. Chomu must have realized that her absence from his home was likely to be permanent, and was probably embarrassed. Joyappa concluded that he overcompensated by boasting and talking about practically any subject with great authority.

Chomu was telling Joyappa that the fertilizer regime he had devised and used last year would yield a coffee crop that was three times the national average. Then Chomu claimed that he had developed a new method of pruning that would boost yields even further next year. Joyappa listened patiently for a while, then put on his dark glasses and took a nap. Since the roads were bad, Joyappa's head kept bobbing around so that Chomu thought his passenger was nodding in response to his monologue.

About an hour later, Chomu pulled in to the parking lot at the site of the tournament. It was the first time the friends had been to this venue. It was a pretty area. The playing fields were surrounded by the hills of the Western Ghats. There were three such fields where matches were proceeding simultaneously. The playing surfaces had been levelled and rolled carefully. Yet, the blazing sun and frequent matches caused the grounds to be coated with reddish dust.

A carnivalesque atmosphere was prevalent at the venue. Little children ran around looking for ice cream and popcorn. Sponsors had put up booths to display their wares. Salespeople talked incessantly as they hawked a wide array of goods ranging from kitchen equipment to farm machinery.

The friends made their way to ground 'A', where Joyappa's family was to play in a few minutes. Chomu's family was scheduled to play their first match two days later on the same ground. As Joyappa walked up to the players to wish them luck, he was intercepted by Nanju, the coach. Nanju, a pleasant sixty-ish fellow with no knowledge of the game, walked up to him with a worried look and said, 'Joya, I am not sure what we are going to do. Two of our players have not made it. They are having car trouble and will not reach in time. If we don't have eleven players, we will have to forfeit the match and that will look very bad.'

'That's not good,' agreed Joyappa. 'Aren't there any youngsters you can rope in until the regular players arrive?'

'No. Not really. I've asked my grandson and granddaughter—they're with us for their summer holidays. But they live in the US and really don't know anything about hockey,' said Nanju, as he pointed to a couple of teenagers standing nearby.

The boy was a strapping young fellow with a massive neck that would not have looked out of place on a bison. The young girl was slim and pretty. She was attired in a pair of white shorts and a tank top. She also wore lots of makeup and a bored look as she chewed gum and gazed into the distance.

'My grandson, Neel, plays American football, and has agreed to give it a shot. He tells me that he's good at baseball too. Anita refuses to play. She says she is a cheerleader in high school and wouldn't want to break a nail,' said Nanju, helplessly.

'Pleeease, Joya, would you play for a while at least? I know Susheela said you should not play, but try to stay on the field for a while and I'll convince my granddaughter to come on as a substitute if you are too tired. Please, Joya—just this one time,' implored the coach.

Joyappa was torn between fear of what Susheela would say if she knew he had played, and a strong desire to help the family. Chomu finally tipped the scale by saying, 'Yeah, Joya. Why don't you play? Susheela need not know.'

'Fine,' said Joyappa after a while. 'Let's do it. Get me a jersey, some shorts and a stick, and I'll try to play for as long as I can.'

Chomu wished Joyappa luck and went to the stands with the other spectators. Joyappa went behind a conveniently located bush and pulled on the team jersey and shorts. He stretched a bit. Since it was so hot, he decided against warming up by jogging. He also used the opportunity to take a look at his teammates. He had to admit that if appearances were anything by which to judge a team, his family squad was not going to intimidate anybody. Other than two athletic-looking youngsters in their early twenties, there were some boys and girls, and a couple of bespectacled men of about forty whose lower bodies attested to the fact that they spent much of their working lives in the chairs of their offices. Then, there was Neel—grandson of the coach—who bulged out of the jersey, and would certainly intimidate the opposing team with his sheer bulk. Joyappa was pleased to know that the goalkeeper *was* a good player, for a sound defence was vital to winning (or avoiding public humiliation).

Before they went on to the field, Joyappa gathered his teammates around and gave them a little pep talk. As there were not enough team jerseys to go around, Anita—who was now officially a substitute—stood next to her brother in her tank top and examined her nails. Joyappa assigned the players various positions. He made sure that Neel would play full-back. He asked the players to play hard, not to be nervous and to stick to their assignments. Then the coach said a little prayer and Joyappa led the team to the ground.

The opposing team was already on the field, hitting balls towards their goalkeeper. Coach Nanju told Joyappa that their captain, Madapa, was the player to watch out for. Madapa had represented the state hockey team, and rumour had it that a berth on the national team was imminent.

When summoned by the referee, Joyappa and the opposing captain trotted over to the centre of the field for the coin toss.

Madapa looked fit, slim and athletic. In contrast, Joyappa's stomach bulged over his waistband, and his man breasts pushed against the jersey. Joyappa's legs were quite hairy, except for the area below his knees which were scarred and hairless from his having scratched at flea bites. The fleas in question were an unintended gift from his pet cats, Tiny and Bug, who loved to curl up and take naps on him.

The captains shook hands and Joyappa was struck by how cocky the young man was. Joyappa called heads and won the toss. The official wished the captains good luck and asked them to play the game in the right spirit.

As soon as the official's back was turned, Madapa snarled, 'That's the only thing you're going to win, you old lump.'

Joyappa fought the urge to grab the young fellow in a head lock and beat him senseless. Instead, he said, 'Oh, we'll see about that, you skinny little nitwit.' Then he added innocently, 'By the way, your fly is undone. And, I'm surprised anyone can play with *such* a small hockey stick.'

When Madapa hurriedly glanced down, everything appeared to be in order. He seethed when he looked up and found Joyappa giggling at him. It was admittedly a juvenile trick, but it left Joyappa amused at his own wit.

III

As matches go, it was not a great one. There were lots of missed balls, poor trapping and inadvertent fouls. Joyappa played centre-forward and was well covered by Madapa, who appeared to be everywhere. He seemed to dribble past the opposition at will, but had trouble getting past the imposing figure of Neel. Then, about fifteen minutes into the game, Neel happened to trip and Madapa used the opportunity to get into the 'D' and fire one past the keeper.

Joyappa was annoyed. He trotted back to Neel and said, 'So, son, is American football a girl's sport?'

'Hell, no!' yelled Neel, his face turning red at the insult.

'Then don't let that fellow get past you, or we will put you in a skirt instead of shorts,' said Joyappa, nastily.

Neel was furious. He gripped the stick so hard that his knuckles turned white and the veins in his massive forearms began to bulge.

'Fine,' said the young man through gritted teeth. 'I'll make sure the guy doesn't get past me.'

Joyappa headed to the centre of the field. As the score was announced over the loudspeaker, Madapa smirked at Joyappa.

Joyappa was annoyed. Madapa cheekily pointed at Joyappa's hockey stick and said, 'Hey, *Ajja*, why don't you use that thing as a walking stick? With you as captain, I'm going to score at least half a dozen.'

Joyappa was struggling with the heat, his poor cardiovascular fitness, and the knee he had injured years ago. Yet, Madapa's behaviour ignited his competitive spirit. He made a couple of lumbering runs and was able to penetrate the opponents' defence, but try as he did, he could not get a single shot on goal. *A little support from my teammates would be nice*, he thought.

About five minutes later, a loose ball rolled towards Neel. He was still furious at Joyappa's comments. Not familiar with the nuances of the game, he just decided to make a clearance instead of passing or dribbling his way up the field. Neel swung his stick and a mighty crack was heard as he made contact with the ball. The opposing centre forward made an effort to trap the ball. He did get a stick on it, but Neel's hit was so powerful that the stick twisted in his hand and the ball flew up in the air. Madapa, who was lurking nearby hoping for another chance to score, leapt to avoid getting hit. The ball hurtled between his legs and eventually crashed into the boards at the opposite end of the ground. In fact, the ball had travelled with such velocity that had Madapa not jumped, his voice may have risen an octave.

Madapa's face turned pale. He was shaken. Winning was important to him, but he wasn't sure if it was worth being maimed. Thereafter, Madapa was cautious about getting too close to Neel. However, he still played a fine game and distributed the ball quite effectively to his teammates.

Young Neel was growing in confidence. A little later, he managed to intercept a pass meant for the opposing centre forward and made a clearance. Madapa's teammates tried to stop the ball. But it was struck so ferociously that no one could trap it cleanly. Finally, after a couple of deflections, the ball happened to reach Joyappa, who was bent over near the opponents' goal post or 'D' trying to catch his breath. Joyappa couldn't believe his luck. He quickly collected the ball, effortlessly (and illegally) shouldered aside the opposing fullback and shot the ball past the goalie. The official, not having seen Joyappa shove the defender aside, blew his whistle and pointed to the centre of the ground. *Joyappa had equalized!*

With the scores level, Joyappa's family members in the stands started screaming with joy. He thought of raising his arms aloft, but was too tired to do so. But he *wasn't* too tired (or immature) to smirk at Madapa, stick his tongue out and say, 'I guess you can't cover me, Mr State Player.'

Joyappa heard cries of 'C'mon, Uncle,' 'Great goal, Joya!' and one young girl even screamed, 'Nice goal, *Thatha*!'

Joyappa was happy to have scored. But he was less thrilled to be addressed as '*Thatha*' or Grandpa.

At half-time, honours were even with the scoreboard reading 1-1. During the break, Joyappa consumed huge amounts of water and swallowed some glucose powder that Coach Nanju offered him. The coach had been worried that the team would be down by half a dozen goals or more midway through the contest. So he was pleased with the score, and especially happy that his grandson, Neel, was doing a good job of scaring the living daylights out of the opposition.

Joyappa's team began to play with more confidence. Madapa, wary of Neel's bulk and power, seemed to play a more defensive role. He was clearly losing his cool and had begun to yell at his teammates. *So much the better for us*, thought Joyappa.

With more faith in his goalie and the defence, Joyappa began to hang around the opposition goal, waiting for an opportunity. Truth be told, he was also too tired to run back and forth. About ten minutes before the final whistle, the right winger made a fine run and centred the ball towards the opponents' goal. Joyappa's eyes opened wide, but as he limped and hopped forward, he knew that he was a step slow and would not reach the ball.

Fate, however, intervened. Madapa, instead of keeping his eye on the ball, was looking for an opportunity to get back at Joyappa. He slyly shoved Joyappa from behind. Joyappa lost his balance and fell down. As expected, his belly made contact with the ground first and he skidded helplessly forward. His arms and legs were outstretched and a cloud of red dust followed his sliding body. Quite by accident (although he would never admit it to anyone), his hockey stick made contact with the ball, which ricocheted off the surprised goalie's pads and crossed the goal line. Joyappa's momentum was such that he, too, continued past the goal line and only stopped when his head slammed against the boards.

Joyappa had scored again! The stands erupted as everyone cheered his heroics. Unfortunately, Joyappa was still stunned and had to be carried off the field. Madapa's dirty play had been observed by the official, so he was shown a card and ejected for the rest of the game.

Coach Nanju was thrilled that his team was ahead. Joyappa, however, was too groggy to play any further. So, with some help from Chomu (who had come down from the stands reeking of beer), the coach peeled the jersey off his semi-conscious centre forward's body. He looked over at his granddaughter. Anita was busy fiddling with her smart phone, apparently oblivious to the drama going on around her. The coach quickly squeezed out as much liquid as he could from the sweat-saturated jersey and walked over to Anita.

'Anitu, sweetie, we need you to go in and play.'

'I really don't feel like getting all sweaty, Nanju *Thatha*,' said Anita as she continued to swipe her fingers across the screen of her phone.

'Please, child, all you would have to do is grab a hockey stick and go and stand behind your brother.'

'Okay, *Thatha*, I guess I could that,' said Anita. 'Remember, I really don't wanna break any nails.'

'You won't break any nails. But before you go on the field,

just slip this jersey on—tournament rules, you know,' said the coach as he handed the young woman Joyappa's jersey.

'It smells kinda funny, *Thatha*. And why's it *wet*?'

'Oh, it is a tradition that we give players who come off the bench wet jerseys, sweetie,' lied Coach Nanju, desperately trying to look sincere. 'You know it will keep your body cool in this heat.'

So Anita finally complied with her grandpa's request, slipped on the sweat-soaked garment, picked up a hockey stick (by the wrong end) and jogged on to the field. She was a pretty girl and had nice legs, so the young men in the stands cheered lustily for her. Anita loved the attention and considered doing a split, but decided against performing her favourite cheerleading move since she didn't want her shorts to get dusty. Instead, she waved at the spectators just as she had seen beauty queens acknowledge cheering crowds on TV.

The few remaining minutes passed uneventfully as neither team was able to score. The game ended shortly thereafter with Joyappa's family having won by a score of 2-1. Madapa left in a huff, badly miffed that he had been sent off the field and his team had lost. Joyappa gradually regained full use of his faculties and appeared none the worse for wear—except for a rapidly swelling lump between the eyes.

When young Anita came off the field at the end of the game, she saw Joyappa sitting up with his upper body exposed and chest hair matted with sweat. His face, in addition to the ugly bump, had a most unusual colour resulting from a mixture of blood, red dust, sweat and powdered glucose. Anita may not have been a theoretical physicist, but she was not stupid. She put two and two together and realized that she was wearing this strange, hairy man's *used* jersey. *So the wetness of the jersey was from man sweat!*

'*Eww, Gross!*' squealed Anita in disgust. '*OMG. Hairy guy sweat. Gag!*' she added, before dramatically throwing off the jersey, charging behind a conveniently located bush and throwing up.

IV

A wealthy industrialist visiting from Delhi, who belonged to Joyappa's clan, had watched the match and was so thrilled at the outcome that he offered to take the team and all of the team's supporters to tea.

Predictably, as the food was free, most people ate heartily. Everyone was in high spirits after the unexpected victory, and Joyappa basked in the glory of having scored both the equalizer and the match winning goal.

Joyappa, who had picked some ice from an ice cream cart earlier, wrapped it in a sock and held it against his injured face during the meal. The injury had clearly not affected his appetite since both he and Chomu happily put away four masala dosas each, and washed them down with strong filter coffee. Neel, the defensive wall, was ingesting his sixth masala dosa, and looked like he was just getting started. However, his sister, Anita, looked pale and upset. She wouldn't eat or drink, but just glared angrily at her grandfather. To be fair, one could not really fault her.

On the drive back, Chomu began to sing a somewhat vulgar song about a pretty girl and her physical assets. Joyappa tried to join in, but his head hurt too much. When Chomu was done singing, he proceeded to tell Joyappa about a new breed of citrus that he had created by crossing a pomelo with a lime. The resulting fruit, according to Chomu, was an enormous lime with improved flavour characteristics. Joyappa slipped on his sunglasses with some difficulty, since the bump between his eyes was quite prominent. Then, he dozed off until Chomu dropped him home.

Joyappa entered the house to find Susheela watching a romantic drama on TV. She occasionally dabbed at her eyes with a handkerchief.

Joyappa said, 'Hello, Susheela. I'm going to take a quick shower. I'll be back shortly.'

'See you soon, dear,' said Susheela with a suppressed sob. Normally, she had to coax or threaten her husband into taking a shower. But she was completely immersed in the movie, and didn't even notice anything odd about Joyappa's sudden interest in personal hygiene.

Joyappa showered thoroughly and removed most of the evidence of the hockey match. As he toweled himself dry, he looked in the mirror and was shocked to see that the bump on his forehead was still obvious, and had actually swelled even more. When he sat next to Susheela on the couch, the movie was over and Susheela was still shedding tears. She gave him a watery smile, hugged him and said, 'So did you have a nice day, Joy?'

'Oh! It wasn't too bad,' he said, which was an understatement. Scoring a couple of goals, hearing the crowd cheer him on, humiliating that cocky Madapa from the opposing team and receiving a lot of praise from his family members had made it a *very* special day. Plus, the oily masala dosas were a bonus.

'Chomu drove me around in his new car. It's really nice,'

continued Joyappa. 'But enough about me, did *you* have a good day?'

'But what happened to your forehead, Joy?' said Susheela, sounding worried as she wiped away a tear and observed the ugly swelling on her husband's face.

'I got out of Chomu's car and happened to bump my head on a piece of wood,' said Joyappa, quite honestly. Then to change the subject, he asked his wife about the movie she was watching.

'It was a great movie, Joy. I'd love to watch it with you sometime,' said Susheela. 'If you like, I'll tell you the story— except for the ending, since I don't want to spoil it for you.'

'Fine,' said Joyappa. 'Do you mind if I turn the TV to the sports channel for a second, while you tell me the story?'

'Sure, dear,' said Susheela before she started to tell him about the movie in great detail. Joyappa was glad that Susheela seemed to have bought his explanation for the bump on his head. He grabbed the remote control and began to change channels on the TV with blinding speed. When he found a professional wrestling channel, he watched (with mouth agape) four large people pulverize each other in a ring.

Joyappa did a superb job of multitasking as Susheela talked about the movie. He pretended to listen to her, and at what he hoped were the right times, grunted and said, 'Really?', 'Is that so?', or, 'That's incredible!' He just prayed that he had dodged a bullet and his wife would never find out about the hockey match.

Eventually, Susheela finished her story, and looking again at the ugly lump on her husband's forehead, said, 'Gosh! Let me get you some ice, Joy.'

'Okay, Susheela,' said Joyappa, 'and some of that pista ice cream would be really nice.'

'Sure, Joy. It will just be a minute.'

Susheela made her way to the kitchen and prepared a cold compress by wrapping some ice in a towel. After placing it on Joyappa's forehead, she felt a little guilty about having prattled on about her movie instead of treating the injury right away. So she dished up an extra large serving of pistachio ice cream for him.

Just then, Susheela's phone buzzed. It was a message from her friend, Asha, with a couple of attachments.

'Congrats, Sue. Great game. Hope the hero is OK.'

Susheela was puzzled. But when she opened the attachments, her friend's cryptic message became crystal clear. First, there was an action photograph of Joyappa on a hockey field. He was sweating profusely and appeared to be shouldering a much smaller person aside. The second photograph showed Joyappa lying on his back just outside the sidelines of a hockey ground. Chomu and an older man appeared to be in the process of removing his jersey. He seemed to be comatose. His sweaty body was smeared with red dust, and there was a bump between his eyes.

Susheela was absolutely furious. All the tender, emotional feelings from her movie evaporated. The urge to stab her husband with a fork on his swollen forehead was very strong. But she took a deep breath, and sat down for a minute to calm herself.

'Oh, Susheeelaa. I'm feeling a bit hot, now. How 'bout that ice cream, dear?' whined Joyappa impatiently from the living room.

Susheela got up and went towards her husband, who was still intensely focused on the TV screen as a big *blonde* man sat on the chest of an equally big *bald* man and bent his victim's legs to an impossible angle.

'Ah, there you are,' said Joyappa without turning around, as he heard Susheela enter the room.

'Here's your ice cream, you BIG, FAT, LIAR!' screamed Susheela. Then, she dumped the bowl and its contents on Joyappa's head, and stormed out of the room.

Joyappa was shocked. The bowl was now perched on his head like a cap. As the green ice cream dripped down his face, he licked it greedily and muttered, 'She could have at least given me a spoon.'

3

Charlie Goes Bride-hunting

I

Joyappa had the house to himself. Susheela would be away for at least a few hours. She was performing one of her noble acts at a nearby village by tutoring underprivileged children for their upcoming school exams—on a volunteer basis, of course.

Joyappa sat on the couch that Sunday afternoon, enjoying a movie. On his left sat Tiny, washing her face as cats are wont to, while Bug, sprawled on his lap, purred as she intently watched the action on the television screen.

The movie was an old Western. *A band of outlaws had kidnapped two young girls somewhere in the northwestern United States. Fortunately for the girls, and unfortunately for the kidnappers, The Careywood Kid was hot on their trail.*

Joyappa's eyes were riveted to the screen. As The Careywood Kid opened fire in one scene, Joyappa felt a rush of adrenaline. He swiftly picked up the two cats and, using them as imaginary guns, began to 'shoot' them at a couple of Susheela's potted palms. The cats, liking any attention, tolerated being treated as revolvers; however, they did glance at each other before turning to look pityingly at their owner.

The shrill ring of his mobile phone interrupted Joyappa's fantasy. He dropped the cats and rummaged for the phone in his pocket.

'Is that Joya?' said a high-pitched, familiar voice.

'Yes, Aunty,' said Joyappa. He stood up upon recognizing the commanding voice of Gangavva, the mother of his good friend, Charlie. He immediately felt like an eleven-year-old schoolboy who had just been caught stealing oranges from a neighbour's orchard.

'I've got something important to discuss with you, Joya. It's about Charlie. He's away playing hockey with some boys in the village. Why don't you and Susheela come by in an hour and join me for tea?'

'I'll be there soon, Aunty,' said Joyappa, still standing at attention. 'But Susheela is doing some volunteer work and won't return until evening.'

What a pity, thought Gangavva. She was of the opinion that Susheela was blessed with most of the couple's grey matter and all of its common sense. 'Why don't you come alone then?'

Joyappa drove his old jeep to Gangavva's place. He touched her feet and sat down at the dining table eagerly. His eagerness stemmed from the fact that Gangavva was an excellent cook who knew nothing about the strict diet mandated by Susheela. His tea started with some delicious pumpkin halwa, made with ghee. Then, he wolfed down half a dozen freshly steamed jackfruit *kolé puttus* slathered with melted ghee. Like most good cooks, Gangavva appreciated the enthusiasm with which her food was being devoured. She kept plying Joyappa with more food and did not disturb him by talking too much. Joyappa finally demolished several soft, buttery *chakkulis* and washed it all down with some very sweet tea.

Gangavva's demeanour and tone of voice might have resembled that of a drill sergeant, but Joyappa knew that a good heart lurked under the tough exterior. Gangavva had realized years ago that her son, Charlie, and his friends were nice enough young men even if they were not intellectual heavyweights. She was well aware that the chances of Charlie (or his pals) having to deliver a Nobel Prize acceptance speech were remote. In fact, the chances of an Indian beating Usain Bolt in a 100 metre sprint were greater than that. It just *wasn't* going to happen— not even if '*naati ota*' (a race through muddy, water-logged paddy fields) was an Olympic event and Bolt's lane was filled with angry crabs. Consequently, she kept her discussion with Joyappa short and to the point.

'Joya, I think it is time my Charlie settled down.'

'Huh?' said Joyappa, puzzled.

Realising that she would have to be even more direct, she said, 'I want Charlie to be married. She should be a good girl from a good family, and must have some brains.' She was too loyal to her son to say that Charlie needed someone intelligent to keep him in line.

'Yes, Aunty,' said Joyappa. He was not sure what was expected of him.

'I'm sure you know Dechi, my cousin's wife's niece. Dechi tells me that her friend's brother, Muddu, knows of an eligible girl who is distantly related to them. The girl's name is Neelamma. I believe they call her Neeli. She just finished her masters, and was a year ahead of Muddu in college. Dechi thinks she would like to get married soon. Although they haven't sent us a formal "offer" for my boy, I think Charlie should meet her.'

Joyappa looked lost, as he was still trying to figure out Dechi's identity. After all, his body was too busy metabolizing all the food that he had just put away, and his brain wasn't at its sharpest.

Observing Joyappa's blank look, Gangavva decided to be as blunt as possible, 'Tomorrow, I would like you to take Charlie to Dechi's place. Neeli will be there. She is visiting from Bangalore. Joya, please give me your opinion of the young woman. But first, let's see if she and Charlie like each other.'

'Okay, Aunty,' said Joyappa with a smile. He thought he understood.

'I'll send some oranges with Charlie for Dechi. That way the purpose of your trip won't be obvious. Also, if I ask Dechi and her husband to be away for a while, maybe Charlie and you can meet Neeli without too many distractions.'

'Yes, Aunty,' said Joyappa.

'I'll send Charlie over to your place at about nine o'clock tomorrow morning. I hope things work out for him, son. And remember to be discreet because Neeli will not know why you're visiting.'

'I'll do my best,' promised Joyappa dutifully, before he drove home in a thoughtful frame of mind. He was preoccupied with his thoughts. He still could not figure out how Muddu, who Gangavva had referred to, was connected to Dechi.

II

That evening, Joyappa explained the situation to Susheela and asked if she would accompany him on the trip to meet the girl. First, Susheela told him that he should not refer to the prospective bride as a 'girl'. If she was over eighteen, then 'young woman' would be more appropriate. Next, Susheela said that she had another class scheduled for that morning, so she would not be able to go. Although Susheela wished Charlie well, privately she said a little prayer for whoever he married.

Joyappa spent a restless night. He was thoroughly confused and worried about several questions—some certainly valid, others irrelevant. What was the relationship between Muddu and Dechi? Was the young woman named Sheila or Leela or Neela? What if Charlie liked the young woman but she didn't care for Charlie? Did the boring oat porridge that he was forced to consume every morning really reduce cholesterol levels? What the heck is cholesterol? He felt a headache coming on before he finally fell asleep.

After Joyappa had finished his breakfast the following morning, he picked up the newspaper and stretched out on the window seat in the dining room. Joyappa seldom read the paper, but as he waited for Charlie, he thought he would brush up on current events. So he started with the important stuff—the sports page. He first looked at the pictures for a couple of minutes. Next, he began reading the flowery prose describing a cricket match. The rest of the world may have discarded this style of writing about fifty years ago, but the journalist seemed completely unaware of that fact. He used long words and highly convoluted sentences that made Joyappa's head spin. So he turned to the cartoons, which elicited a couple of giggles. Joyappa didn't even bother with what he considered the boring stuff—politics, conflicts in the Middle East, global warming, deforestation, El Niño, etc. Within five minutes of having occupied the couch, Joyappa resembled a log—a hairy, snoring, paunchy sort of log.

Joyappa did not hear the knock on the front door. Susheela, who was two rooms away, did. She opened the door and just stared. She did not recognize the visitor. For one thing, the morning sun was in her eyes. Also, she had never seen *anyone* attired like the person before her.

The visitor smiled, revealing tobacco stained teeth and said, 'Hello, Sush.'

Susheela hated being called Sush, but she was too confused to reprimand the visitor. The voice was familiar, and slowly recognition dawned on her.

'Come in, Charlie,' she said, shakily.

As Charlie entered, Susheela coughed and her face turned red—one cannot be sure if it was mirth or just surprise that prompted her discomfiture. Charlie offered to get a glass of water, but Susheela declined by shaking her head.

Charlie had undergone a transformation since she saw him last. He seemed to have stepped out of a Hindi movie from the '70s. Since Susheela didn't watch Hindi movies, she had never encountered fashion of this nature. His hair was cut so that it resembled an oily helmet that covered his ears. The once lush moustache had been trimmed to a wispy thread just above his upper lip. His shirt was pale pink covered with dark blue paisleys. The top two buttons had been left undone revealing a thin gold chain nestling in a bed of hair. His long legs were encased in high-waisted, dazzlingly white flared pants. The shirt and pants were made of some sort of shiny synthetic material that was completely devoid of cotton. Charlie's ensemble was completed by chunky, black patent leather platform shoes.

Susheela motioned to Charlie to have a seat and shook Joyappa awake. She went into the kitchen, stuffed a napkin in her mouth and laughed until tears ran down her face.

Charlie sat down and waited for Joyappa. Tiny had been sunning herself in the window. As the cat hadn't seen Charlie for a while, she hopped onto his lap, apparently undeterred by his new appearance. Charlie scratched her under the chin and she began to purr. Soon, Tiny rolled over and Charlie made cooing noises as he scratched her belly. The love fest was interrupted by the entry of Joyappa. Charlie gently deposited the cat on the floor and rose to greet his friend.

'Charrrleee,' said Joyappa in greeting. Like a good friend, he did not bat an eye at his pal's sartorial sense. Or perhaps he simply approved of Charlie's style, and wished he had the freedom to dress like his friend.

'What's new, Joya?' replied Charlie, pleased to see his pal.

Joyappa decided that he would drive, as Charlie might be nervous. So he took the keys to Charlie's pick-up truck and they set off towards Dechi's place. Charlie looked pale and was not particularly communicative during the drive. So, Joyappa decided to discuss the miserable state of Indian hockey to get Charlie's mind off his impending meeting. His plan worked for a while, and the friends spent several minutes criticizing the selection policy, the lack of facilities in the country, and the apathy of both the media and public about what was once considered the national sport. But as they neared their destination, Charlie fell silent and began to gnaw at his fingernails.

Joyappa drove up the driveway lined with crotons and

parked near the house. As planned, Dechi and her husband had left half an hour earlier. The house, with a colourful, manicured garden in front, was old, and exuded character. Joyappa got out of the car and lifted the oranges out of the back of the vehicle. Charlie was a little slow at alighting, but he finally emerged on wobbly legs.

'Come on, Charlie. You'll be fine,' said Joyappa, encouragingly.

Charlie attempted to smile, but his nerves got the better of him and he suddenly charged for the nearest ornamental bush (which happened to be an *Ixora*) and began to vomit copiously. As Charlie straightened, he glanced down and was horrified to see that his once pristine white pants had apparently sprouted several dark hairs in the vicinity of his groin. He almost screamed in fear before realizing that Joyappa's cat had shed her fur all over his lap. Charlie proceeded to vigorously brush the cat hair from his pants, when the front door of the house opened. A young woman walked out to the verandah. Even Charlie was sensitive enough to realize that his frenzied activity was hardly likely to create a favourable impression on a prospective bride, so he stopped immediately.

Joyappa tried to divert the young woman's attention by loudly bellowing, 'Hello, Hello, Hello. Is Dechi home?'

'Hello,' said the young woman, clearly not sure of what to make of the visitors. It is a definite credit to her courage that she didn't close the door and barricade herself inside after what she had just witnessed.

'Dechi isn't home. You are...?'

'I'm Joyappa and this is her cousin, Charlie. We're here to drop off some oranges, so we hoped to see her.'

'I'm Neeli,' said the young woman. 'She should be back shortly. Please come and sit down.'

Joyappa deposited the box of oranges on the verandah and the two friends sat down opposite Neeli. Charlie, aware that there were still some stray cat hairs adhering to his pants, crossed his legs. He hoped the offending hair wouldn't be visible. When he regained his composure, he tuned in to the conversation between Joyappa and Neeli, which had moved from the state of the weather to the poor performance by the Indian hockey team.

Joyappa casually asked Neeli where she was from and if she was working. The young woman said that she was based in Bangalore and was a painter. Charlie didn't say much—he was still very nervous—but he observed Neeli with an intensity that a tiger might display before pouncing on a spotted deer. He decided that he had not seen a more beautiful woman in his life.

She was tall, with smooth, dark skin and delicate features. Her silky hair was long and cascaded well past her shoulders. For the life of him, Charlie could not understand the preoccupation with fairness and fairness creams. He personally found dark skin and long hair very appealing. Presently, Neeli rose to get the visitors some tea. She wore tightly fitting, faded jeans, torn slightly at the knees and a white cotton shirt with the sleeves rolled up. To Charlie, she seemed to move with the grace of a gazelle. Clearly, he was well and truly smitten.

While Neeli was away, Charlie gave Joyappa a thumbs up before removing the remaining cat hairs from his pants. The young woman returned with some tea and brownies for the visitors. As Joyappa devoured the brownies, Charlie's scrutiny of Neeli continued. Now, his examination was as intent and thorough as that of a scientist studying every cell of a newly discovered organism under a microscope.

Neeli sported small, elegant silver earrings, shaped like spiders. Around her neck, she wore a large, silver pendant suspended from a string of small wooden beads. Charlie decided that too intent a study of the necklace (or its attractive surroundings) may not be appropriate, but he did conclude that the pendant resembled a scorpion with its tail raised to strike.

He also noticed that Neeli's attire was much more casual than that of Susheela or her friends, and he quite liked the style. Most importantly, Neeli seemed to have a kind face. He also liked the slightly husky sound of her voice and her frequent laughter.

This, thought Charlie, *is the girl for me.*

After tea, the two friends took leave of Neeli. Charlie walked to the pick-up truck with the swagger of a young John Travolta in *Saturday Night Fever*. His polyester clothes certainly suited the walk. On the drive back, he was most loquacious. All he could talk about was Neeli.

When they reached Joyappa's place, Susheela was out in the garden pruning the roses, having just returned from her class. Charlie was normally wary of Susheela, but love had infused him with courage and he gave her a 'high five' that almost sprained her wrist.

'Well, how did it go?' asked Susheela as she massaged her wrist.

'Oh! Sush, she's just fantastic,' gushed Charlie, and proceeded to rhapsodize about Neeli's beauty, her sense of style, her ability to brew the perfect cup of tea, and so on.

Susheela winced when she was addressed as 'Sush', and

exercised great self-control to keep from grabbing Charlie by the ears and twisting until he squealed like a pig. Both Joyappa and Susheela were happy to see Charlie so excited, but they also didn't want him to get hurt. Most importantly, no one knew what Neeli thought of Charlie. Several questions were at the tip of Susheela's tongue. When Charlie finally paused for breath, she decided to verbalize some of her concerns.

'Charlie, do you really think Neeli would want to leave the city for a secluded rural existence?' asked Susheela. 'You've seen the way city people complain about problems here. They can't adapt to the frequent power outages, lack of entertainment and career opportunities, bad roads, insects, lizards, snakes and elephants. How do you know if the young woman even likes this area?'

'C'mon, Sush. She's a painter, for one thing. So there will be plenty of work every year. Everyone wants their house painted after the monsoon.'

Susheela rolled her eyes in exasperation, 'I don't think she's a *house* painter, Charlie. She's probably an artist.'

'*Ohhhhh!*' said both Charlie and Joyappa in unison. Charlie's spirits weren't easily dampened, and he said, 'Well, there's a lot of stuff she can paint. After all, it *is* a very pretty area with lots of wildlife and mountains and things.'

'That's true,' said Susheela, thoughtfully.

'And,' said Charlie triumphantly, 'she likes insects—she had jewellery in the shape of spiders and scorpions.'

Clearly, Charlie had slept through his biology classes in school. Susheela decided not to get into the differences between arachnids and insects. But, she was impressed that Charlie was finally enthusiastic about something worthwhile, instead of the debauchery that, in her mind, characterized his lifestyle.

Susheela decided that given the general ineptitude of her husband and his friend, she would have to get involved. Joyappa noticed that familiar determined look in her eye when she put the pruning shears in her pocket and said, 'Okay, fellows. Let's make this thing happen. We've got a *lot* of work to do.'

As they trooped into the house for lunch, Charlie sported a lovesick grin. Joyappa's spirits lifted, because when Susheela set her mind to something—she invariably succeeded.

4

Susheela Takes Charge

I

Susheela got to work right away. She decided that she needed to meet the young woman who had captured Charlie's fancy. The day after Charlie and Joyappa met Neeli, Susheela baked some pastries and drove over to Dechi's place. By design, she arrived less than an hour before lunch and was detained for the meal. As part of her evaluation, Susheela sat opposite the unsuspecting Neeli, who she discreetly questioned and observed during lunch.

When Susheela returned home that afternoon, she was in a pensive frame of mind. Joyappa was sitting in a comfortable armchair struggling to read a sports magazine. While Susheela was away, he had drunk most of a bottle of cooking wine that he had found in the kitchen and had diluted the remaining liquor so the volume of liquid remained unaltered, although it now appeared pink instead of red. He was having a hard time keeping his eyes open.

'I just met Neeli,' said Susheela.

'Hmmm,' replied her husband, barely suppressing a yawn. 'Well, Joy, what did you think of her?'

Joyappa's senses were instantly on high alert, for it was a question fraught with peril. He had actually quite liked the young woman and concurred with Charlie about her attractiveness. However, from long experience, he knew that he could easily end up in hot water if he was too complimentary about another woman's attributes. If he was honest with Susheela, he would have said that Neeli was a stunner. However, in the interests of domestic harmony, he yawned, then casually said, 'I thought she was okay,' before pretending to read his magazine.

'That's not really an answer,' said Susheela.

'Is that a vehicle coming up the drive?' said Joyappa, in an effort to change the topic.

Susheela cocked her head to the side and said, 'No, I don't think so. I don't hear a thing.'

'It must have been something travelling on the main road. Wasn't the weather pleasant today?'

Susheela decided that it would be pointless to prolong this line of questioning. She wondered, not for the first time, if her husband had been dropped on his head as a baby.

'Yes, Joy. The weather was nice,' she said, through gritted teeth. 'Well, *I* think that woman is an absolute knockout.'

'Did you know that Iron Mike Tyson *knocked out* a number of his opponents in his early fights?' said Joyappa.

'She's beautiful *and* intelligent,' continued Susheela. 'But, I am not sure if I agree with her sense of style—what's with the torn jeans and that weird jewellery? It all seems a bit Bohemian to me.'

'I hope it rains,' said Joyappa. 'A light shower would be nice.'

'She might actually be good for Charlie,' said Susheela thoughtfully, completely ignoring Joyappa's unrelated babbling.

II

Two days had elapsed since Joyappa and Charlie met Neeli— two days during which Charlie moped around like a lovesick fool. Susheela had a plan in place and she knew that a lot of hard work would be required to carry it through. First, Charlie would have to be cleaned up. However tolerant Neeli might be, it was clear to Susheela that Charlie would require a major makeover.

Susheela called Brinda's Beautique, one of the better salons in town. As a rule, men were not allowed in this haven for women. Susheela coaxed and cajoled, but the owner of the salon was adamant that no male would enter the establishment.

Finally, as with any major negotiation, a compromise was reached. In exchange for a large amount of money and a promise from Susheela that she would direct all her friends to the salon, the owner agreed to allow a team of her best employees to 'clean up' Charlie. The operation would be conducted after official working hours and all participants would be sworn to secrecy.

Later that evening, when visibility was poor, Susheela seated Charlie in her compact car. Charlie had to fold his long legs so his knees were pressed against the dashboard. During the drive to the salon, his head often made violent contact with the roof of the car. Unmindful of the physical discomfort, the poor besotted fellow just stared out of the window with glassy eyes.

Susheela parked just outside the back door of the salon.

No lights were visible as the curtains and blinds were closed. Susheela knocked twice, waited fifteen seconds and knocked again three times. The door was opened by Brinda herself. Susheela quickly pushed Charlie in, before entering herself. Charlie looked around in puzzlement at the feminine decor, not quite sure what was happening. Brinda studied Charlie for a couple of minutes with a practiced eye, shook her head and began to whisper to Susheela.

Charlie thought he heard Brinda say, 'Please, Madam. I don't think it will even be possible.'

He saw Susheela open her purse and a large amount of money changed hands. Then Brinda, looking very worried, said, 'Okay, Madam. For you, I will try but I am not sure what the girls will say.'

Susheela said, 'Follow her, Charlie. Remember, it is for your own good.'

'Okay, Sush,' said Charlie, trustingly.

Brinda asked Charlie to leave his worn leather jacket in the waiting area before she took him by the arm and led him to another room. As Susheela seated herself in the waiting area and picked up a fashion magazine, a quarter bottle of cheap brandy slipped out of the pocket of Charlie's jacket and fell on the carpeted floor. Susheela shook her head in disgust, picked up the bottle and put it back in the pocket.

Four of Brinda's employees were already waiting for Charlie. These women were specialists in their respective fields. After one look at their customer, they realized that 'Operation Charlie' was undoubtedly the greatest beauty challenge they had ever encountered. However, being professionals, they put their game faces on and steeled themselves for the trial ahead.

Before Charlie was treated to a 'facial', an electric razor was deployed to shave his beard and the wispy moustache. The rest of the undesirable hair on his face was removed by threading and plucking, before a range of treatments was employed to remove the blackheads, pimples and long-term deposits of dirt.

Next, Charlie's ultra greasy hair had to be washed. Brinda sincerely hoped the oily effluent wouldn't clog her sink. It was only after four separate washing and rinsing cycles that the hair was deemed suitable for cutting. Susheela had asked that Charlie's hair be styled into something more contemporary. Anticipating protests by their customer, all mirrors in the room were covered and Charlie was given a haircut that Susheela had chosen from one of her fashion magazines. One young woman then donned a pair of surgical gloves and began to clip the thick tufts of hair that grew out of Charlie's ears and nostrils. Charlie didn't protest, but he did giggle a few times since his ears tended to be a bit ticklish.

The next order of business was a manicure, followed by a pedicure. The older woman in charge of the treatment was taken aback at the gnarled, discoloured nails, callused hands and the heels covered with dry, cracked skin. Despite soaking Charlie's feet in water, two of her clippers broke when she tried to cut his toe nails. Luckily, she wasn't daunted by the setback. She asked one of her junior colleagues to run over to the local pet store to get some nail clippers meant for large dogs. Following a prolonged soak in water supplemented with various additives, much scrubbing and the use of the Great Dane nail clippers, Charlie's hands and feet were transformed into a moderately presentable state.

Charlie was then led to another room and asked to remove

his shirt. After he was directed to lie face down on a padded table in the centre of the room, the bright lights located directly above were turned on. There was a sudden and collective *whoosh* of indrawn breath at the sight the women beheld—the dense mass of coarse black hair covering Charlie's shoulders and back was unlike anything they had seen before. Remarkably, the thick pelt was actually visible all the way from the bony shoulders down to the belt holding up the faded, low-rise jeans.

Brinda, who specialized in removal of unwanted body hair, was not to be deterred. She picked up a big jar of pre-warmed, sticky, viscous material and slathered it across Charlie's exposed back. Before the next step, the four beauticians took hold of Charlie's arms and legs. Expecting a pleasant massage, Charlie relaxed his body. Brinda spread a piece of fabric over the areas covered with wax, pressed down and quickly pulled the cloth up.

There was a ripping sound as a thick mass of hair was detached from Charlie's back. Charlie screamed and strained to free himself, but to no avail. His limbs were firmly held down and he could not escape.

'*Avvaya, Aiyyo!*' screamed Charlie.

Susheela, who was engrossed in an article about anti-ageing lotions, rose abruptly. Again, there was a ripping sound followed by a loud scream from Charlie, '*Aiyyo, Sush! Help me. Please.*'

Susheela jammed her fingers in her ears, but she could not block the sound of Charlie's desperate screams. Being addressed as 'Sush' grated, but the tortured wailing touched a chord. She considered leaving the building and sitting in her car, until she heard a horrible sob and a pathetic, 'Oh God! *Sivane*! *Dammayya* Sush.'

So Susheela reluctantly entered the room where Charlie was being treated. She saw her husband's friend being held down by a determined set of women. Charlie's lower back looked raw and hairless, with little drops of blood emerging from the waxed areas. The rest of the back and his bony shoulders still sported lush black hair.

Charlie was blubbering like a baby and alternately saying, 'Help! Mummy,' and 'Pleeease, Sush,' as one young woman wiped the mixture of tears and other fluids from his face.

Susheela felt bad. When she had ordered a back-waxing, she had no idea that Brinda would have to denude what seemed like several acres of tropical rainforest. 'Brinda, isn't there *something* you can do? He seems to be in a lot of pain,' said Susheela.

'Madam,' said Brinda, as sweat poured down the sides of her face, 'What to do? Do you think this is an easy job? We're doing the best we can. I'm beginning to wonder if we even have enough wax in the shop. I've assembled a crack team but we have never, ever had to do anything like this.'

Susheela's eyes strayed to the top of Charlie's low-rise jeans and sympathized with the 'crack' team. Obviously, she could not very well halt the procedure and leave Charlie with half a hairy back. Fortunately, she had watched a number of romantic movies set during the American Civil War. So she was well aware that in that era, doctors often performed amputations and other major surgeries in the field with no anesthesia.

Susheela acted swiftly and decisively. She rushed out of the room, fished out the bottle of brandy from Charlie's jacket and returned to the 'operation theatre'. She patted Charlie on his head and said, 'There, there. It will be okay, Charlie. This will make you feel better,' as she inserted a straw into the bottle and held it to his lips. Despite still being held down by the beauticians, Charlie imbibed all of the undiluted liquor in a remarkably short time.

Susheela then grabbed the nearest object she could find, which happened to be a hair brush. She shoved it in Charlie's mouth and he clamped down on the wooden handle. Confident now that he would not bite off his tongue, Susheela left the room to resume reading about anti-ageing creams.

An hour later, Charlie emerged, shining like a newly minted, if slightly droopy, rupee coin. Susheela thanked the exhausted team profusely and willingly parted with another small fortune. As she drove Charlie home, she was distinctly uncomfortable to be at the receiving end of her passenger's accusing looks. She felt like she had taken an unsuspecting pup to the vet's to be neutered. Although Susheela was happy with the result, she was wracked with guilt, as she was not sure if it was morally right to alter the natural state of an animal.

'I was proud of my back hair,' said Charlie, sadly. 'I was the first boy in my entire class in school to grow body hair.'

'Hmm,' said Susheela.

'Don't you think it is manly to have hair on one's back, Sush?' said Charlie.

Susheela pretended not to hear. She turned on the stereo system and cranked up the volume to preclude any further awkward discussion.

III

Over the next few days, Susheela ordered some smart new clothes over the Internet. Predictably, Charlie's new feathers didn't fit just right, so they were altered by a local tailor to meet Susheela's exacting standards. She also dragged Charlie to the dentist. Mercifully, it was not a painful experience for Charlie, although the dentist struggled for hours to clean and polish the tobacco-stained teeth.

Since Susheela wanted Charlie to have at least a passing knowledge of art, she asked him to read various books on the Old Masters, Mughal miniatures and contemporary Oriental and Western artists. She hoped that he would then be able to carry out an intelligent conversation with Neeli. Overall, she was pleased with Charlie's progress, although he tended to linger for inordinately long periods on depictions of nude women.

Susheela also gave Charlie a crash course in etiquette. She insisted that he raise his eyes and make eye-contact while talking to a woman, instead of focusing with laser-like intensity on other areas. Surprisingly, Charlie was quite receptive to Susheela's efforts and made significant progress. Susheela was pleased, as it revealed the depth of his emotions for Neeli. But the big question remained—would Neeli feel the same way as Charlie?

IV

Susheela wanted Neeli to meet the new and improved Charlie. But as she didn't want to be too obvious, Susheela made a few secret phone calls to Dechi, and together they hatched a plan. Much to Joyappa's chagrin, he was made part of this scheme. He would have preferred to spend his day off watching an old Western on TV and drinking beer on the sly, but Susheela bribed him with an offer he could not refuse—she promised to cook him a meal of crisp *akki otti* and *pandi* curry for the night. Plus, he *did* want to help Charlie.

Dechi and Neelamma were to attend a wedding in a nearby

town on Sunday. Susheela provided Charlie and Joyappa with
a light brunch. The unsuspecting Charlie was then 'prepared'
for the day. As a precautionary measure, Joyappa locked up the
cats as he didn't want them shedding their hair all over Charlie's
pants again. Charlie was attired in grey trousers and an off-white
cotton shirt. His feet were encased in dark socks and matching
suede loafers. A dark blue single-breasted blazer completed the
ensemble. Susheela sprayed him with something from a bottle,
flicked an imaginary speck of dust from his lapel, and stepped
back to look at him with her head cocked to one side.

She smiled in approval and addressed Joyappa, 'Well, I
think he looks very handsome. What do you think, Joy?'

Joyappa looked at the tall, clean shaven figure in front of
him. He felt a little sad, since the person looked nothing like
his old friend. Wisely, he kept his counsel and said, 'Yes, he
looks very smart. Very different from before, though.'

'Yes, Joy. *Very, very* different,' said Susheela with a pleased
smile.

It was an absolutely beautiful afternoon. The sun was out,
yet there was a slight nip in the air. Doves cooed, woodpeckers
banged away in the distance, insects made assorted sounds and
the air was fragrant with the smell of flowers. Joyappa drove
with Susheela by his side, while Charlie sat at the back. The
weather was so pleasant that Susheela actually refrained from
criticizing Joyappa's driving. Instead, she periodically squeezed
his hand with affection. Even Charlie, encased for days in his
love-sick cocoon, felt a tiny bit of pleasure at the sight of a
sambar doe nuzzling her fawn at the edge of the forest.

Susheela directed Joyappa to a new bookstore in town.
Attached to the bookstore was a swanky coffee shop that

served dozens of different concoctions. Joyappa looked at the prices and was peeved to realize that the coffee was marked up hundreds of times from what the grower was paid. Yet, there was no denying that the atmosphere was pleasant and the padded chairs were comfortable and inviting. When Susheela wandered off to look for a book, Joyappa examined the pastries displayed in a glass case near the espresso machine. Charlie was lost in his thoughts as he stared out of a large French window that overlooked the colourful little garden outside.

After a quarter of an hour, during which Charlie had changed neither his position nor his expression, a couple of new customers walked in. Susheela paid for her purchases and walked over with a smile to meet Dechi and Neeli, who had just attended a wedding.

Dechi, who looked a bit tense, was dressed conventionally in a shimmering blue silk sari with a gold border. She also wore traditional gold jewelry. Neeli, on the other hand, wore an unusual purple sari covered with a beetle motif. The sari was pinned at the shoulder with a brooch in the shape of a large rhinoceros beetle, while her smooth brown arms were bare except for a simple silver bracelet with a beetle-shaped clasp. Neeli's glossy black hair was pulled back in a French braid, accentuating a pair of plain silver hoop earings.

When Susheela saw Neeli's attire, she froze momentarily, and her eyes went blinkety-blink. People who knew her well would have realized that the blinking signified disapproval. She might not have appreciated Neeli's unconventional sense of style, but she had to admit that she looked quite stunning.

'What a surprise to see you here,' lied Dechi.

'Yes, I *know!*' said Susheela, equally untruthfully. She

managed to stop blinking and force a smile as she gestured towards Joyappa and Charlie and said, 'My husband and a friend are here and we were just looking for something to read.'

They all turned towards Joyappa, who was crouched over the glass case reading the pastry labels. If Charlie was looking for something to read, it must have been located outside the store, as he stared out of the window.

'Why don't you join us for some coffee?' said Susheela.

'That sounds good, doesn't it, Neeli?' said Dechi.

'Yes, I could go for a cappuccino,' said Neeli.

Susheela pried Joyappa away from his scrutiny of the pastries. In the meanwhile, Dechi, noticing Charlie's zombie-like state, went up to him, patted him on the back and said, cheerfully but somewhat untruthfully, 'Hi, Charlie! You're looking well.'

Charlie appeared so flaccid and lifeless that, if he were a plant, any competent horticulturist would have concluded that he had reached his 'permanent wilting point'. He acknowledged Dechi with a sad and unenthusiastic wave and mumbled, 'HihowareyouDech?'

Dechi took Charlie by the arm and directed him to the table where Susheela, Joyappa and Neeli were already seated. When Charlie saw Neeli, the change in his demeanour couldn't have been more dramatic. He seemed to quickly return to the land of the living. A horticulturist, or even a casual observer, would have been astounded at the instantaneous reversal of his wilted state.

As he greeted Neeli, Charlie fortunately remembered Susheela's instructions and maintained eye contact. He smiled for the first time in days, dazzling one and all with his polished, super-white teeth.

Neeli looked a little puzzled when she saw Charlie, before recognition gradually dawned on her. 'Hello! You look a bit different,' she said to Charlie, and then added mischievously, 'I hope you've got over your nausea.'

Charlie had the grace to look embarrassed, as he was unaware that Neeli had observed his inadvertent fertilization of an *Ixora* bush during his visit to Dechi's house. However, he was so happy to see her that his discomfiture did not last for long.

Susheela ordered a round of gourmet Italian coffees for everyone except Joyappa, who had to be content with a cup of high-grown green tea. Afterwards, Susheela caught Dechi's eye and said, 'Oh, I just remembered—Joy has an appointment with his dentist. Dechi, didn't you say you wanted to see a dentist some time?'

'Oh, that's right. I'd like to come with you Susheela, if that's okay.'

'Sure. Maybe Charlie and Neeli can wait here instead of wasting time in the dentist's office. We'll be back soon. I hope the two of you don't mind.'

'Nope, nope, not at all. Don't mind, Sush. Don't mind one bit,' said Charlie, quickly.

'Good,' said Susheela. 'I'm sure they have a lot of books that might interest you,' she said.

As Joyappa settled the exorbitant bill, Susheela noted with concern that he was gritting his teeth so hard that he might *actually* require the services of a dentist.

V

Unfortunately for poor Joyappa, who detested having to visit any medical facility, Susheela did indeed leave him in the tender care of a local dentist for a quick checkup, while she and Dechi shopped for groceries. About an hour later, they all returned to the bookstore.

Neeli and Charlie were seated side by side on a couch with a book titled 'History of Art' in front of them. The book was opened to a page with a beautiful impressionist painting by Edouard Manet. Neeli was discussing the painting, while Charlie nodded and appeared to be paying attention. Susheela was relieved. She was half expecting to see Neeli's face approximating *The Scream* by Munch after an hour with Charlie.

'Hello,' said Dechi with a smile, 'I hope the two of you weren't too bored.'

Neeli looked up and said, 'No, not at all. Charlie and I were just discussing art.'

Joyappa, who was still grumpy and feeling violated after the dentist had scraped and poked around in his oral cavity, looked surprised. Dechi looked very pleased as she exchanged looks with Susheela.

'Charlie, you ready to go, man?' asked Joyappa, who was anxious to get home. He wanted Susheela to have enough time to properly season the pork she had promised to cook for him. He also hoped to sneak away to the garage with Charlie and have some much needed beer that he had concealed there.

'Okay, Joya. Neeli just finished telling me about the difference between Manet's and Monet's painting styles,' said Charlie.

Susheela resisted the urge to say, 'I think he's got it! By George, he's got it!'

In contrast, Joyappa restrained himself from clubbing Charlie over the head. The change in his friend was shocking. What had happened to the guy who typically stared crudely at any young woman and kept girly magazines (and more) under his mattress? What was this art and '*Monay-molay*' rubbish he was talking about?

Dechi was feeling much more relaxed, now. When Susheela had called a few days ago, she had agreed to the rendezvous with some trepidation. Although she had always liked Charlie, Dechi felt that he used to look unkempt and had questionable taste in clothes. Also, rumours abounded that respectable families tended to lock up their marriageable daughters if he was in the vicinity. But clearly, he must have just been in a rebellious phase. She wondered how someone, who looked so clean-cut and had an interest in fine art, could have acquired such a bad reputation. He was *such* a nice fellow—well dressed, with *really* nice teeth and was ever so polite. He seemed perfect for Neeli, she concluded. She resolved to call the young woman's parents that evening to tell them that she had found someone suitable for their daughter.

As they rose from the couch, Charlie said, 'By the way, Sush...' He stopped abruptly as Susheela began to blink. Then he continued after correcting himself, 'Susheela, would you and Joya come over to our place tomorrow for lunch? I hear that Dechi will be away for the day and as Neeli will be alone, I thought she could come and meet my mother.'

Susheela nodded in agreement. Joyappa quickly said, 'We'll be there, Charlie.' He wasn't going to pass up the opportunity to feast on Charlie's mother's cooking. He hoped she would make that special pepper fried mutton that he loved. Her meatball curry was special, too.

In the parking lot outside, Susheela noticed that there was a glow to Neeli's face that had not been apparent earlier in the afternoon. Also, there was no mistaking the tender look that came into her eyes every time she gazed at Charlie. As Joyappa followed Dechi's car out of the parking lot, Charlie and Neeli kept waving to each other.

Susheela felt her master plan working. She was sure that a match had been made.

5

Joyappa Takes a Hike

I

Joyappa was finishing his breakfast. He stuffed a piece of bone-dry toast in his mouth and somehow managed to force it down. Normally, he was permitted marmalade, jam or something that would lubricate his gullet, but that privilege had been withdrawn. Concerned that his cholesterol and blood sugar were at unacceptable levels, his wife, Susheela, had made his diet more stringent than usual.

It was Saturday, and Joyappa would have to pay his estate employees that evening. Actually, Susheela did all of the calculations and even counted out the money. All Joyappa would have to do was look important and distribute the cash.

Joyappa was really looking forward to this particular Sunday. Susheela had planned an excursion with some of her fellow nature-loving friends, and Joyappa anticipated a relaxed time with no spousal supervision. He had it all worked out in his head. After Susheela left, he intended to watch the final day of a cricket Test match that was tantalizingly poised. He had already hidden away several bottles of beer in the garage. If his pals, Charlie and Chomu, were free, he would invite them over, and they were bound to have a grand time. A victory for the Indian cricket team would be icing on the cake.

Susheela sat across from Joyappa and did not appear to be happy. Although earlier that morning she had been in a pleasant mood, after she spent a quarter of an hour doing something on her laptop, her disposition had changed for the worse. Joyappa wasn't sure what had happened, but when she returned, she seemed to be displeased about something. Joyappa wondered if Susheela had just received the result of his most recent blood test via e-mail. Perhaps his cholesterol levels had increased since the last test. Whatever the reason for her grumpy mood, he was uncomfortable under the cold and penetrating gaze of his wife.

Joyappa's attention span tended to be short. So, thoughts of the relaxed Sunday he had planned soon alleviated his discomfort. When he thought Susheela wasn't watching, he dipped his dry toast into some tea, and quickly put the soggy mess in his mouth. He had to carry out this operation surreptitiously since Susheela found this habit disgusting and thought it constituted poor table manners.

As Joyappa rose after drinking his tea, Susheela smiled at him. Joyappa may not have been a rocket scientist, but he was perceptive enough to know that the smile hadn't reached his wife's eyes. He became a bit nervous.

'Oh Joy, *darling*,' said Susheela sweetly, 'if you've got a minute, I'd like to show you something.'

'Okay,' said Joy, feeling more nervous. People knowledgeable in the ways of the jungle say that deer can often sense that they are being stalked by a predator and take evasive action. Similarly, Joyappa's sixth sense told him that no good things were likely to happen in the immediate future. His instincts were right, but there was to be no escaping his fate.

Joyappa followed his wife into the little study. Susheela sat down at her desk.

'*Honey*,' said Susheela. 'Do you remember, some time ago you came home feeling unwell after I asked you to supervise work on the Forest Block of the estate?'

'Unngh,' grunted Joyappa warily, not sure where the conversation was going.

'Well, my friend Jo told me that she saw you that day in Mysore with some rough-looking characters. I informed her in no uncertain terms that she was imagining things, and that you were supervising work all day.'

Joyappa didn't even bother to grunt—he was seriously worried.

'Jo, as I'm sure you recall, is a professor and was busy with teaching or evaluating exam scripts until last week. But she's somewhat free now, and as she was removing unwanted photographs from her camera phone, she found something quite interesting.'

Susheela flipped open her laptop and asked Joyappa to come closer. Joyappa walked over to the desk with all the enthusiasm of a man scheduled to face a firing squad. The gentle sound of the laptop booting up was as menacing to Joyappa as the sound of guns being cocked by the executioners. Susheela pulled up a photograph and the image filled the screen. At the bottom of the screen, Joyappa observed the date and time that the photograph was taken. The image itself showed him walking down a street followed by his friends, Charlie and Chomu. Joyappa's gut looked enormous and the top button of his jeans was undone. All three men had mouths stained red by paan. It was a good action shot, even if the subjects were not the prettiest, since Chomu could be seen spitting out a stream of red liquid into a nearby drain.

Joyappa turned pale and his mouth went dry. He considered falling to the ground and feigning a heart-attack to get out of trouble. But he couldn't quite remember if the heart was located on the left or right of one's chest—so he dropped the idea. Next, he considered faking an inflamed appendix—but again, he wasn't sure exactly on which side of his body it was located. Clutching the wrong side of his abdomen would only add to his embarrassment. Evidently, there was nothing to do but face the music.

Susheela had stopped pretending to be friendly. Her eyes were cold and hard. The ambient temperature in the study seemed to have abruptly plummeted. Given the incriminating evidence on her computer screen, questioning Joyappa would have been pointless. For his part, Joyappa didn't even think of mounting a defense. He just avoided making eye contact with Susheela and waited for his sentence to be pronounced.

'Tomorrow, as you know, I am going on a trek with my friends through some wild terrain,' said Susheela. 'You, Joyappa, will pick up all of the people on this list, and accompany us. You will be the only man present, and you will be required to carry our refreshments. So, tomorrow morning, be ready at 5.00 a.m. *Sharp!*'

Joyappa, his dreams for Sunday shattered, turned and slunk out of the room. *Going fifteen rounds with Mike Tyson would be preferable*, he thought, *to a whole day with Susheela's friends.*

II

The following morning, Susheela shook her snoring husband awake. Despite the early hour, Susheela was already dressed in trendy outdoor clothes and fashionable hiking boots. Before she left to prepare some sandwiches for the outing, she told Joyappa, 'You had better dress properly. A long sleeved green shirt and those camouflage pants I got you would be appropriate. I think the terrain is pretty rough, so put on your hiking boots, too. Also, you should carry a jacket and a change of clothes—just in case.'

'Hmmm,' said Joyappa sleepily. He wondered just who she thought she was advising about the outdoors? *Did she think he was a novice, a city slicker, or a complete idiot?* It was fortuitous that he did not wonder aloud, because he would not have been happy with Susheela's answer.

Joyappa was in a slightly rebellious mood. His Sunday plans had been destroyed. So he decided to deliberately disregard Susheela's advice and to dress comfortably. He wore a bright red tee-shirt that a younger cousin had given him that said 'Las Vegas' in neon green letters on the front. Since he found the shirt a little constricting, he ripped the sleeves off to give it a rugged look. He decided to wear shorts instead of camouflage pants. He had put on weight since he last wore them, yet he stubbornly forced them on. They were too tight, too short, and accentuated his prominent stomach. Figuring that heavy hiking boots would be uncomfortable, Joyappa slipped on a pair of thin canvas shoes with no socks.

Since Susheela didn't have time to cook that morning,

Joyappa made himself a bowl of corn flakes with cold milk and a cup of tea (from a tea bag). It was sustenance, but it wasn't what his palate craved.

Susheela was already seated in their jeep and was evidently still upset about the incriminating photograph that her friend had sent. She had packed sandwiches, chips and assorted fruits for the trip. When Joyappa started the jeep, she didn't even bother to glance at him. She just stared straight ahead.

Joyappa drove to several different houses to pick up Susheela's hiking friends. There were eight women, including Susheela. There was Mo (Mohini), Axa (Accava), Jammy (Jamuna), Vinnie (Vinita), Annie (Anita), Gangsy (Gangamma) and of course, Ash (Asha). They were all remarkably well-groomed, considering it was so early in the day, and attired in expensive hiking apparel.

Joyappa watched and listened to his wife interacting with her friends. He was astounded at the contrast between the way he was being shunned and the effusive greetings, childish giggling and 'mwah mwahs' that Susheela bestowed on her pals. Only Gangamma, who was the nicest of the lot in Joyappa's opinion, actually smiled at him and enquired about his health. The rest of the women barely acknowledged his existence. He guessed that Susheela had told Asha about his clandestine trip with his friends and the related photographic evidence, because she gave him a look—the kind of withering, contemptuous glare that would have made a full grown tiger slink away with its tail between its legs.

By the time the little group reached the vast private sanctuary where they planned to trek, Joyappa was furious. *I'll show them*, he thought. *I'll show those snooty, half-starved women how a real man hikes, and they will be sorry. I'll walk so fast that they won't be able to keep up with me, and then they'll give me the respect I deserve.*

III

Joyappa pulled in to a large grassy meadow within the sanctuary, and parked the jeep. Susheela and her friends had obtained special permission to spend the day in the area. The weather was perfect for hiking. There was a slight nip in the air, and although the sanctuary typically received very high levels of precipitation, it promised to be a clear day. The proposed route for the day's hike went through some wetlands, followed by a gradual ascent through dense 'shola' forest characteristic of the Western Ghats, up to the rocky summit. The descent would be carried out along a different, considerably steeper path that led back to the field where Joyappa's vehicle was parked.

Susheela added some desserts, that either Vinnie or Mo had baked, to the haversack containing the fruit and sandwiches. She looked meaningfully at Joyappa without uttering a word. Joyappa sauntered over and picked up the haversack. It was heavier than he expected. For the first time, his fellow hikers, including Susheela, saw Joyappa's outfit in all its glory. The giggling and chatter stopped abruptly as they observed Joyappa's too-tight, too-short shorts, crudely ripped tee-shirt and the abundance of dense, dark body hair that covered almost every inch of exposed skin.

Joyappa was aware of the sudden silence. He was proud of his thick, powerful thighs and massive calves. Assuming (and it was a bold assumption) that the women were admiring his legs, he strutted across the field towards a path leading through a swampy area.

Susheela followed Joyappa, while the rest of the women walked in single file behind her along the narrow path. She heard some whispering and giggling from some of the younger women. Among other things, she did hear some stray words including 'grizzly,' 'gorilla' and 'orangutan'. Since the Western Ghats do not constitute the natural habitat of the aforementioned animals, Susheela guessed who the words referred to, and her face burned. Meanwhile, as Joyappa proudly strode ahead of the others, he attempted to suck in his gut, which resulted in his prominent rear end protruding even more than usual.

Joyappa was motoring along at a good pace. Yet, the women behind him had no problem keeping up; after all, these were people who did all sorts of things to maintain their youthful figures. Many of them sweated (they would say, perspired) through rigorous physical activity that often included aerobics, yoga, jogging, cross-training, squash and tennis. Plus, they watched what they ate.

Some ten minutes into the hike, Joyappa began to find the going tough. His cheap canvas shoes got stuck in the soggy wetland mud several times. Since he was leading the little group, he ran into several spider webs that added to his discomfiture.

With great effort, Joyappa increased his pace and created a bit of separation from the rest of the pack. After struggling through the swampy area, he began to climb up a gentle slope with vegetation along the sides of the trail. Since he was wearing shorts, his legs were constantly brushing against the knee-high plants, which included stinging nettles. Consequently, Joyappa began to feel an itchy, burning sensation in his legs. He turned around to find that his companions were unaffected by this problem, as they were all clad in pants. He gritted his teeth and continued to walk.

Despite the early hour, Joyappa had begun to sweat copiously and his decidedly skimpy outfit provided ample opportunity for hungry mosquitoes to feast. He kept slapping the unclothed parts of his body (of which there were vast expanses) in an effort to kill the insects. The women behind looked at him curiously. He sourly speculated that all the cosmetics on the women probably kept the mosquitoes at bay.

The rapid pace left Joyappa winded. He decided that he needed a break, so he stepped to the side of the narrow trail and pretended to tie his shoelaces. Susheela walked by as if he did not exist. When Asha passed him with no expression on her face, he thought he felt a blast of air from the frozen wastelands of Siberia—laced with some expensive French perfume. The rest of the women also overtook him. Except for Gangamma, who smiled pleasantly, no one so much as glanced his way.

Joyappa was too tired to feel offended. He was just glad for the break. At that point he would have cheerfully given a kidney for a cold beer and a cigarette. After he had retied his shoelaces for the fifth time, Joyappa decided to push on. When he did not see any sign of the others after several minutes, he became concerned.

Joyappa struggled along for another half hour. His manly pride was wounded and he increased his pace with great effort. Sweat poured off his body and he could feel blisters forming on his feet. As he rounded a bend, he heard the sound of female voices along with the gentle murmur of flowing water. Shortly, he came upon a clear mountain stream running between several smooth black rocks. The banks of the stream were lined with assorted ferns. The branches of several trees leaned over the stream and filtered the sunlight so it danced across the moving water. It was a gorgeous spot, but Joyappa was too fatigued to appreciate its beauty.

Some of the women sat on the banks, with their bare feet in the water. A few of the younger ones were wading and playing in the clear water. Joyappa had no idea how the young women had the energy to frolic after walking uphill for so long.

All Joyappa wanted to do was throw off his cheap canvas shoes and immerse himself in the cool water. Yet, he had his pride. So with great self-control, he forced himself to keep walking. He crossed the stream by stepping from rock to rock and continued along the trail. Eventually, he came across a pretty little waterfall that probably fed the stream below. He looked around, and seeing no one behind him, decided that this was an opportunity he just could not pass up. So, he set the haversack aside and stood under the waterfall fully clothed. He gasped as the cool water washed across his overheated, sweaty body. Following the torture to which his body (and mind) had been subjected, the water felt wonderful. He opened his mouth and quenched his thirst, hoping fervently that no one had performed unsanitary acts upstream.

Joyappa felt greatly refreshed, but he knew that he would feel even better if the cool mountain water had access to his entire body. So he removed his shoes, pulled off his clothes and threw them aside. As the water coursed over his naked body, he felt like he was in heaven. *He* clearly felt good as he splashed around happily; however, the scene was not one to be viewed by the faint of heart. The lone monkey observing Joyappa from a *Terminalia* tree was curious, but appeared not to be revolted by the hairy person in the water.

After the initial euphoria, Joyappa realized that Susheela and her pals would make an appearance soon. He quickly donned his wet clothes, grabbed the haversack and set off up the hill. By now, Joyappa was feeling pangs of hunger. He knew Susheela had made several sandwiches, but he wasn't sure if she had actually counted them. With great self-control, he managed to keep walking up the hill.

He had now reached the dense forest of the higher elevation. The sun was out, but as the vegetation from the stunted trees provided adequate shade, the heat did not really bother him. After a half an hour of steady walking, he reached a slight clearing in the forest. He looked down and spotted some of the women walking in single file up the hill. Given their superior cardiovascular fitness, he estimated that they would reach the clearing shortly.

Again, Joyappa felt the need for nourishment. He knew that Susheela had made her special chutney as a spread for the sandwiches. He loved the chutney. But he wasn't sure about the filling—egg salad, ham and cheese, roast pork, salami, or...? The suspense was killing him as much as his mounting hunger. He thought he'd just take a look. After all, it wouldn't hurt to know what he was going to eat when they reached the summit.

'I'll just take a peek before we reach the peak,' he said to himself. He actually giggled at his clever word play, not really considering how piqued his wife would be to know of his plan.

The mere thought of food had stimulated Joyappa's salivary glands. His willpower had completely evaporated at this point. There was no going back. Quickly, he undid the haversack and counted out the foil-wrapped sandwiches. He counted twenty nine sandwiches, all neatly packed and marked with different coloured labels.

Joyappa spent the next few minutes trying to figure how many sandwiches would be assigned per person. Mathematics had never been his strong suit in school. Come to think of it, he had struggled with all of his subjects. At any rate, he finally gave up his calculations and decided that one sandwich wouldn't be missed. So, he chose a wrapper with a pink label, extracted a sandwich and bit into it. It was a chicken salad sandwich that was absolutely delicious. Joyappa closed his eyes as he chewed and felt the strength building up in his muscles. Before he knew it, the sandwich was gone. *I really don't think it will be missed,* thought Joyappa.

He was curious about the sandwiches with the blue label. *I'll just take a teeny-weeny look,* thought Joyappa. It was a ham sandwich, and Joyappa did more than just look—he practically inhaled it and concluded that it just might be better than the chicken salad. To cut a long story short, Joyappa also demolished a cucumber and chutney sandwich, an egg salad sandwich and a salami sandwich. He enjoyed every bite, and was forced to undo the topmost button of his shorts. When he was done, he decided that he could not leave the incriminating foil wrappers, so he stuffed them into the back pockets of his shorts. The evidence was hidden, but his rear end protruded even more.

Duly fortified, Joyappa resumed his walk up the trail. Initially, he made good time. As the climb became steeper, he began to huff and puff. He was struggling and his full stomach began to cramp from the exertion. Mercifully, there was still adequate shade and he kept pushing onwards.

Just as he thought he would have to take a breather, a strong odour hit his nostrils. Thanks to Tiny and Bug and their activities, it only took him a few seconds to recognize the smell of cat urine. He guessed there was a tiger or a panther on the prowl, and decided to keep going. Each step was painful and sweat began to pour off his body, yet he wasn't in the mood to be a snack for some hungry feline, so he trudged onward. As he went past the tree line, he blinked as the full force of the sun hit him. He was now only a few hundred metres from the summit. The area was covered with grass and interspersed with several large, unusually-shaped boulders. Every move was now a struggle but Joyappa gamely pushed forward step by agonizing step.

Finally, there was nothing left to scale except for a very large black boulder that, he concluded, was too steep to climb. *Joyappa had done it. He had beaten the uppity women to the top!* His heart swelled with pride. Tossing aside the haversack, which seemed to weigh a ton, he collapsed onto his back and stretched his arms skyward. He fought the urge to scream, 'I'm so haaapy,' like the great Roger Federer after winning Wimbledon.

When his head stopped spinning, and the sweat drained out of his eyes, Joyappa sat up. He thought he heard voices, so he looked around in surprise. There was no one there. Then he looked up and saw two of Susheela's pals, possibly Mo and Vinnie, sitting on top of the black boulder apparently playing cards.

'Hi, Joy,' said Mo from up above. 'What took you so long?'

'You look really tired,' said Vinnie, sweetly, 'We were watching you come up and honestly thought you would collapse.'

'But, but, but….,' said Joyappa, absolutely flabbergasted, and unable to finish his sentence.

The two young women had taken a steeper, more hazardous route, and just for the fun of it scaled the sheer boulder on top of the hill that Joyappa had deemed insurmountable. They had become bored waiting for the rest of the hikers and begun to play some silly card game called 'bluff'.

Now Joyappa's pride was badly wounded. If, after an epic five-set Federer victory, the Duke of Kent had grabbed the Wimbledon trophy from the champion and said, 'Sorry, old chap, that's not for you,' odds are that Roger would be crushed, too. Well, that's just how Joyappa felt, and only iron self-control (or possibly dehydration) prevented him from blubbering like a baby.

IV

Susheela and the rest of the women reached the top of the hill shortly thereafter. The women didn't seem to be particularly tired, and admired the view below them. There were hills with grassy slopes, dense forests, and valleys with acres and acres of paddy fields. Coffee plantations were visible in the distance, interspersed with flowering trees. The orange flowers of the *Spathodea* trees and the bright yellow *Cassia* blooms formed a dramatic splash of colour against the many shades of green.

Joyappa sat away from the women, sulking. The magnificent view was lost on him. Having been beaten to the top was frustrating to Joyappa. He wished he was home with his cats. At least they liked him unconditionally. Brooding, he hung his head between his knees. Unfortunately, this led to another crisis as he noticed splashes of blood on his legs. He looked harder and realized that several leeches were nourishing themselves at his expense. He wished he could burn the little blood suckers off, but he had not brought along any cigarettes for obvious reasons. So he began to carefully part the hair on his legs and remove the hungrily feasting parasites.

He heard Mo and Vinnie giggling, and he thought he heard Vinnie say, 'Looks like he's tatting.'

Mo said, 'Nope. Probably crocheting,' and the giggles turned into full fledged laughter.

Joyappa didn't know what they meant, so he ignored them and continued to detach leeches from various parts of his anatomy.

Susheela was readying the meal for everyone. She was not the head-scratching type, but she looked puzzled when she saw the number of sandwiches in the haversack. *I must have made fewer sandwiches than I planned*, she thought. Nevertheless, there appeared to be enough food for everyone, so she began to distribute the sandwiches with Gangamma's help. She pointedly avoided offering Joyappa any food.

Gangamma, however, walked up to Joyappa and pleasantly said, 'Thanks for lugging all that food up the hill, Joy. You must be tired and hungry.'

'It was no problem, Gangamma. I'm not hungry after that short walk. And anyway, I'm not a particularly big eater,' lied Joyappa.

Upon overhearing Joyappa's statement, Susheela, whose back was towards them, rolled her eyes in disbelief. She knew that left unchecked, Joyappa often made a pig of himself. She was torn between wanting to scoff at her husband's statement and genuine concern about his lack of appetite. As she was still very angry with Joyappa, she decided to continue to ignore him.

'Go ahead, Joy,' said Gangamma encouragingly, 'there should be plenty of food for everyone. Here, why don't you have three sandwiches?'

'Okay, Gangamma, if you insist, I guess I could try and force myself to eat something,' said Joyappa as he quickly picked up the sandwiches. The women were nibbling at their own food, so no one was observing Joyappa. For someone who had just stated that he wasn't hungry, Joyappa did a remarkably good job of making the sandwiches disappear. Next, he quickly polished off a couple of brownies, a muffin and some banana bread. He felt much, much better after the meal.

Joyappa stretched out on the grass and dozed off as the women chatted, played cards or admired the scenery. When the women were ready to head back, Vinne threw a pebble at Joyappa as he napped in the shade. The pebble hit Joyappa's distended stomach and bounced off dramatically. Mo and Vinnie giggled. Fortunately, Joyappa woke up before the young women could start a game to see who could get a pebble to bounce the highest off his stomach.

Joyappa guessed that the descent would be easier than the climb up the hill. Mo and Vinne were the first to get on the narrow trail and Joyappa followed closely behind. He planned to shadow the two women and, at the right time, pass them so he was the first person to reach the jeep.

The trail was considerably steeper than the path used for the ascent. Joyappa's cheap canvas shoes provided little purchase and he had to exercise great care to keep from falling down and potentially crushing the young women ahead of him.

Susheela and the others followed at a more sedate pace.

Sunlight glinted off several narrow waterfalls that fed a river in the plains. Some of the women took photographs of the scenery, while others pointed out various landmarks. The wildlife enthusiasts excitedly identified rare birds of the Western Ghats, and argued about whether the pugmarks they spotted were that of a panther or a small tiger.

Joyappa was oblivious to the magnificent view or the interesting flora and fauna. He was completely focused on executing his game plan. He had watched the last Olympics and admired the strategy of a skinny middle distance runner who had conserved his energy by allowing someone else to set the pace, before sneakily blowing past the poor, exhausted fellow over the last lap.

Then everything changed abruptly. Mo, who had been following Vinnie, suddenly lost her footing on a loose stone and briefly went airborne. It was a particularly steep area and she landed heavily on Vinnie's back. Vinnie, in turn, lost her balance and both women came crashing down on the narrow path.

Joyappa was about fifteen metres behind the women when they fell. He briefly considered stepping over and around them. With an effort, he forced himself to stop and do the chivalrous thing by helping the young women up. He was dismayed to find that both Mo and Vinnie were crying.

One of Joyappa's least favourite activities was trying to comfort crying women. He had learnt from bitter experience that if he *didn't* say anything, he would be considered cold and uncaring. He also knew that if he actually *did* speak, he could potentially turn Coorg's Abbey Falls into the mighty Niagara. So he made a weird clicking sound that he hoped sounded sympathetic and said, 'Oh, oh,' in a comforting way as he helped the women to the side of the trail and examined their injuries.

Mo had skinned both knees badly and had a bruise on her chin. Vinnie's injuries seemed to be more serious. Her left ankle was already beginning to swell, so Joyappa carefully removed her hiking boot. He guessed that it was a bad sprain or possibly a fracture. He had personally experienced and seen enough injuries during his hockey career to know that it would be impossible for Vinnie to put any weight on her left foot.

There were no signs of the other hikers, so Joyappa decided to take matters into his own hands. First, he chose a stout stick from the side of the trail and gave it to Mo to use for support. Then he picked up Vinnie, and set off down the trail.

Initially, Joyappa was surprised at how little Vinnie weighed. But as he carefully negotiated the steep, rocky path, she seemed to get heavier and heavier. The going was tough. His arms were burning, his clothes were soaked and Vinnie added to his discomfort by weeping continuously. Fortunately, she was in no condition to observe the copious amounts of sweat that dripped off his face and body onto her, or she might well have decided to crawl home.

The rest of the women caught up with Mo, who was hobbling along with the help of her walking stick. They were very concerned to hear about Vinnie's injury. As they followed the trail, they caught occasional glimpses of Joyappa and Vinnie far below.

For a while, the hikers lost sight of Joyappa as the trail wound its way between two massive black boulders. Several minutes later, Joyappa, still carrying Vinnie, emerged from the shadow of the rocks and began to walk across a flat, open field covered with lush, wild grass. He was headed for a densely wooded area through which the trail passed. By this time, he was absolutely exhausted and in considerable discomfort. The thin canvas shoes had caused painful blisters to form on his feet. The short shorts had allowed his thick thighs to rub against each other as he walked, so the skin felt quite raw. As a result, he was forced to hobble along with his legs apart as if he had a groin infection. Yet, Joyappa soldiered on, concentrating on taking one step at a time.

Suddenly, Gangamma shouted and pointed downwards. It was not Joyappa's awkward gait that prompted her reaction. Gangamma had noticed that a large elephant had emerged from the forest and was advancing slowly towards Joyappa and Vinnie. Joyappa appeared to be unaware of the danger as he trudged on.

'Watch out! Joy,' yelled Susheela, desperate with worry. The other women also joined in and shouted at the top of their lungs. Neither Joyappa nor Vinnie could hear the warning cries, but the women high above kept on yelling loudly. Joyappa just continued to walk along the path with his head lowered.

Everyone had heard of the rogue elephant that had killed several people in a nearby village. Whether the tusker in Joyappa's path was the rogue wasn't known. Nevertheless, approaching a wild elephant on foot was a dangerous proposition under any circumstances. Several of the women began to cry as Joyappa got closer to the dark, menacing bulk of the elephant.

The big tusker flattened his ears and began to advance purposefully towards the strange figure. Susheela and the women high above had stopped yelling and watched in horrified silence.

This did not appear to be a mock charge.

Joyappa looked up and sweat dripped into his eyes. He shook his head and saw what looked like a large swaying tree ahead of him. Unconcerned, he continued to advance with his awkward, wide-legged limp.

The elephant was thoroughly confused to find this odd figure coming straight at him. In his memory, anything he ever charged had run away. He became somewhat tentative, slowed down and stopped. He could now smell the sweat from the advancing figure and noticed that a second human was apparently attached to the first. Finally, the big tusker wheeled around and bolted back to the forest.

Joyappa was close enough to actually feel the ground shake. He wondered if an earthquake was going to add to his problems, but was too tired to care. So he just plodded on with steely determination.

The observers high above began to stir. The colour slowly returned to their pale, frightened faces. Mo had actually swooned and was being supported by Asha. Susheela had to sit down for a minute. Gradually the women, barely able to believe what they had just seen, began to talk.

'I don't think I have ever seen a braver act,' declared Asha. The rest of the women agreed. Soon they began to thank Susheela for having brought along her strong, fearless husband. Susheela smiled wanly, not sure how to respond. The rest of the journey down to the base of the hill was conducted in virtual silence as the women tried to assimilate the remarkable incident they had just witnessed.

When they reached the base of the hill where the jeep was parked, Vinnie was sitting up with her back against a tree and her legs stretched out in front of her. She seemed to be in a lot of pain. Her ankle was swollen and discoloured, but she was now composed. The women first clustered around Vinnie, making sympathetic noises. Gangamma removed her scarf and wrapped it around Vinnie's injured ankle. Next, the women turned their attention to Vinnie's saviour.

The hero was asleep in the shade of a large *Ficus* tree. Joyappa snored gently as he lay sprawled on his back. His limbs twitched occasionally, and the hairs of his moustache fluttered as he exhaled. Susheela nudged him awake. In stark contrast to the way he was treated in the morning, Susheela and her friends clucked and fussed over him. Someone offered him a large muffin and a can of apple juice, both of which were quickly wolfed down.

The infusion of carbohydrates got his brain working again. He understood that the women were appreciative of his efforts in getting their injured friend off the mountain safely. After a while, he also realized that they thought he had chased away a rogue elephant. He had no recollection of any such incident, but enjoyed basking in the adulation of Susheela and her friends.

Asha was particularly warm to him. She smiled sweetly as she felt his biceps and said, 'Gosh, Joy. You must be really strong.'

'Oh, yes.' said Mo, 'He carried Vinnie almost all the way down the hill. He was *so* brave.'

Several of the women hugged him. A few of them kissed him, as well. Susheela felt proud and flattered when Anita, who was married to a bookish, bespectacled scientist, said, 'I wish *my* husband was as strong and brave as yours, Sue.'

'I guess grizzlies have their uses,' said Susheela as she looked pointedly at Mo. Mo's face was flushed with embarrassment.

She wasn't sure where to look, so she began to fuss with her injured knee.

Eventually, they all piled into the jeep. On their way home, a quick visit to a local doctor set everyone's mind at ease. The doctor concluded that Vinnie's ankle was not broken. She had suffered a bad sprain and with some rest, she would be just fine in a couple of weeks. Mo's wounds were disinfected and dressed at the same clinic.

As Joyappa dropped the women home, they thanked him warmly, hugged him and were so effusive in their praise that Susheela felt a twinge of jealousy. Finally, it was just Joyappa and Susheela in the jeep. Joyappa was relieved that Susheela no longer appeared to be angry with him. His mood was buoyant after all the attention he had received. He began to hum tunelessly while drumming his fingers against the steering wheel.

As they drove up to their house, Susheela thought that it was quite remarkable that Joyappa had managed to get through his punishment and come out smelling of roses. Then the wind direction changed, and she wrinkled her nose and muttered to herself, 'Well, maybe not *roses*.'

6

Joyappa Visits the In-laws

I

Susheela's parents lived in the northern part of the district. As far as Joyappa was concerned, the northern part of the country would have been a more suitable location for his in-laws. Actually, the *North Pole* might have worked for him. It wasn't that he had anything against them, but he got the feeling that they just didn't think he was good enough for their daughter.

Fortunately for Joyappa, as the roads of the district had been so badly neglected by the powers-that-be, the drive to the in-laws' home was undertaken only on rare occasions. One such occasion loomed like a dark monsoon cloud over his head.

Susheela's parents were to celebrate their wedding anniversary. The anniversary marked some significant number—Joyappa couldn't remember if the in-laws had been married for twenty five, fifty or a hundred years. He was well aware that Susheela would make his life hell on earth if he chose to avoid the celebrations, so he prepared himself for the ordeal.

Unfortunately for Joyappa, his cats had recently been infested by fleas. The fleas were young, agile, hungry and abundant. Since the cats spent a lot of time on Joyappa, he had also been bitten badly. The fleas had attacked various parts of his anatomy, but seemed to have a special fondness for his ankles and shins. Within hours of being bitten, he began to suffer an allergic reaction. Little red, itchy dots appeared on his body. He knew from past experience that it would be best to avoid scratching these inflamed areas. However, as he packed an overnight bag, the cats began to rub themselves against his legs as if to dissuade him from leaving. The friction caused the little red dots to itch even more and Joyappa was forced to exercise incredible self-control to keep from scratching himself. Another unfortunate consequence of all the feline affection was the new batch of fleas that hopped onto his already irritated ankles.

Predictably, Joyappa panicked. He charged to the bathroom, where he filled a bucket with steaming hot water. He added a generous amount of bleach to the bucket, quickly divested himself of all of his clothes and plunged the garments into the bleach solution.

'Ha! Take that you little blood-suckers,' he shouted.

It is doubtful whether the fleas heard him. Nevertheless, he felt good about his revenge. The good feeling only lasted until a few fleas hiding in his body hair decided to bite him in a place that one wouldn't normally scratch in public. In an ill-advised move, he splashed a little bleach on himself and the sudden stinging sensation elicited an inadvertent squeal.

Joyappa cursed loudly and hoped that Susheela hadn't heard him. He quickly turned on the shower and let hot water run all over his body. It afforded him a lot of relief. In fact, as he let the water run over a particularly itchy spot, Joyappa thought that, physically, this was the best sensation he had ever experienced. Then he thought of another really good feeling—the taste of tender chunks of pork, marinated in assorted spices and cooked over an open flame on a wet monsoon day. Pretty soon, he thought of *yet* another wonderful physical sensation; however, this one could not very well be described in polite company. At this point, Joyappa had trouble deciding which of the feelings was the very best.

The piping hot water made the bites stop itching for a while. Pleased that he had outwitted the fleas, Joyappa changed in to some clean clothes and looked around for his cell phone. He let out a cry of anguish when he realized that the device was in the pocket of the pants that he had immersed in bleach. Frantically, he extracted the phone from his wet pants and turned it on. The screen lit up briefly and began flickering, but would not come on.

Joyappa was distraught. The phone was a gift from Susheela that had been procured at great expense through her cousin based in the US Despite all its fancy features, Joyappa used the phone primarily to talk to his friends, Chomu and Charlie. He hadn't taken the time to figure out the attributes and applications that prompted the manufacturer to advertise the device as the most advanced smart phone available. As the bleached screen flickered one last time before finally dying, he reflected sadly that he was never going to use those features. Since he also knew that he was going to get the mother of all lectures from Susheela, Joyappa decided to postpone informing her of the mishap for as long as he could.

II

The drive to Susheela's parents' house was hard for Joyappa. The condition of the roads caused him to drive carefully as he avoided pot-holes and loose stones. Frequent braking, acceleration and wrestling with the steering wheel caused his clothes to rub against the flea bites. The bites were now angry, red pustules. As the numbing effects of his hot shower wore off, Joyappa's level of discomfort progressively increased.

In the meanwhile, Susheela was in high spirits and prattled on about something. Joyappa, who was struggling with the steering wheel and his pustules, paid even less attention than usual to his wife's conversation. He managed a few grunts, nods, smiles and the odd 'yes' or 'no' and hoped that he wouldn't get into trouble. Two miserable hours later, Joyappa drove up to the gates of his in-laws' property.

The wrought iron gates had been painted black and were set in stone pillars. A black, polished marble slab embedded in one of the pillars bore the name of Susheela's father in gold lettering. Lt. General (retd.) Belliappa's name was followed by what seemed to be half the alphabet. These abbreviations stood for the various awards for gallantry that had been conferred upon the former war hero. Joyappa had no clue as to what the letters represented. He speculated that the initials stood for additional names that the General's parents must have bestowed upon him. Joyappa was glad that his own name was not followed by as many initials. He felt it would be a huge challenge not only to remember what each letter represented, but also to fill out government forms that required the entry of one's full name.

Quite unlike the public roads, the tarred driveway to the bungalow was in good condition. On either side of the drive were flowering trees, including a *Cassia*, a *Spathodea*, different *Tabebuia* species and a leguminous tree with blue flowers that he could not name. The overall effect was pleasing to the eye, although Joyappa could not appreciate the beauty of the trees or the immaculately kept garden. Instead, his stomach tightened as the meeting with Susheela's parents drew closer. In contrast, Susheela was excited and laughed as she related a story about how her 'Daddy' had scared a boy half to death for asking her to the movies when she was a teenager. Joyappa had heard the story several times before. He had failed to see the humour in the story when he first heard it, and found the latest narration even less amusing.

Soon after Joyappa parked outside the bungalow, the polished rosewood doors opened. Susheela squealed with pleasure when she saw her parents. Mother and daughter hugged and kissed, before Susheela launched herself in to her father's arms like a little girl. The old man was tough; he barely winced despite the pain he felt from an old war wound, and managed to retain his ramrod straight posture. Maintaining his composure at seeing his 'little girl', however, posed a greater challenge.

In the meanwhile, Joyappa stood just outside the doors with a cardboard box full of home grown avocados and litchis in his arms. After Susheela and her parents exchanged pleasantries, Joyappa's father-in-law greeted him with tepid, 'Um, hello, there. How are you?'

Joyappa was on the verge of telling him about the terrible itching sensation that afflicted him, but the old man walked away without waiting for a reply.

Susheela's mother's greeting was not much warmer. Her thin lips quivered in a failed attempt to smile as she coldly said, 'Please come in, Joy. Why don't you make your way to the blue bedroom?'

'Hello, hello,' said Joyappa with manufactured cheer, pretending not to be insulted. He deposited the heavy box of fruit in the pantry, and went back to the car for their luggage, which he hauled to the guest room. He collapsed on the bed and decided to take a nap before the big dinner party. Susheela, in the meantime, helped her mother with preparations for the evening.

III

Susheela's mother, Kannu, was from a very wealthy land-owning family. She had inherited the stately old house and a well established plantation of Arabica coffee. Joyappa's father-in-law's origins were more humble. At a time when employment opportunities were scarce, young Bellie had decided to join the armed forces, like many of his contemporaries. At least it meant steady employment, and in his martial community, a career in the army commanded a lot of respect.

◆

Belliappa had been commissioned in an old regiment with a proud history. Consequently, he was often sent to troubled areas along the country's borders. While the chances of getting hurt (or worse) were high, constant action also afforded the young officer valuable combat experience and a chance to move up in the army. Belliappa wasn't a particularly cerebral officer, but there was no questioning his bravery.

One incident in particular sparked Belliappa's meteoric rise to the top (or close to the top) of the armed forces. As part of an exercise, somewhere in the dense jungles of the Northeast, Lieutenant Belliappa trailed a Colonel of his regiment. A couple of scouts had gone ahead, while the rest of the troops followed the officers. Having grown up in a home surrounded by dense rainforests, Belliappa was not uncomfortable in the environment. It was a misty morning and visibility was poor. The odour of decaying vegetation hung heavily in the air. A birdcall rang out a few hundred metres to Belliappa's left. A couple of minutes later, he heard a similar call to his right. Something didn't seem right about the calls. Belliappa's senses were on high-alert, and he closed to within a couple of feet of the Colonel. Later, he could not say what prompted his subsequent actions: perhaps it was the smell of unwashed bodies or the whisper of cloth against the dense undergrowth—but his actions were instinctive and rapid.

Belliappa suddenly knocked the Colonel off his feet. The surprised officer began to swear, when all hell broke loose. The quiet of the jungle was shattered by the roar of gunfire. A bullet, carefully directed by a militant towards the Colonel's heart, hit him in the shoulder instead. Belliappa felt several bullets pluck at his clothes. When he turned around, he saw that the soldier immediately behind him had been shot through the forehead, while another man lay on his back staring sightlessly upwards as blood darkened his shirt. The Colonel began to moan. Belliappa decided that saving the Colonel should be his priority, so he dragged him into the dense undergrowth.

He could now hear his men shooting back at the militants. The ambush had been well planned and executed. The little patrol had been heavily depleted by the initial volley and the remaining troops were on unfamiliar ground. It was unlikely that the scouts who had gone ahead would be found alive. Belliappa guessed that they had been silenced by poison-tipped arrows. The N.C.O. in charge did the right thing by providing covering fire and ordering the troops to retreat to their camp.

The Colonel began to moan again. Belliappa shoved a handkerchief into the wounded man's mouth. As the sound of gunfire faded away, the jungle fell silent again. A few minutes later, he heard the suspicious birdcall from about fifty feet away. An answering sound was heard from nearby. Shortly thereafter, several militants approached the trail to evaluate the results of the ambush. Belliappa heard the militants talking to each other and the sound of laughter. A wounded soldier groaned and a shot rang out to silence him. Belliappa was furious. He fought the desire to lob a grenade at the militants and follow with his gun blazing. But he knew the Colonel's safety was of paramount importance.

The militants relieved the dead troops of anything they deemed useful, from weapons to boots, before leaving. The Colonel was semi-conscious and losing blood. Belliappa ripped off a piece of his shirt to fashion a crude bandage for the injured man's shoulder. With all the activity, Belliappa had not felt any pain, but now he saw that he had been hit on his left arm. Fortunately, it was a flesh wound and did not appear to be too serious. Belliappa bound his own arm to prevent further loss of blood.

Staying away from known trails, Belliappa carried the injured man over his shoulders. It was a tense, nightmarish trek during which the young Lieutenant was well served by the knowledge of the jungle acquired during his youth in the Western Ghats. His arm was stiffening up and beginning to hurt badly. The Colonel kept drifting in and out of consciousness and it took a superhuman effort for Belliappa to keep going. On one occasion, he almost stumbled upon a dozen rough-looking armed men—possibly militants. Fortunately, he was able to avoid them as they sat in a circle, cleaned their weapons and talked in low voices. Finally, when he seemed to have exhausted all his reserves of strength, he was hailed by a sentry at the periphery of the army camp. Exhausted from his efforts and the loss of blood, Belliappa laid the Colonel down before slipping into unconsciousness.

This Colonel was highly regarded in the armed forces and was marked for greater things. News of the young Lieutenant's bravery spread quickly and he found himself being decorated. Belliappa's valour in other troubled areas contributed to additional laurels and a rapid rise up the ranks.

◆

Joyappa was largely unaware of his father-in-law's army career and was not sure why the old soldier was accorded so much respect in the community. His knowledge of military hierarchy was rudimentary; in fact, he thought that the rank of Colonel (which he pronounced *Karrnul*) was one of the highest in the army. He often wondered why several 'Karrnuls' in the district saluted and treated old Lt. General Belliappa with such deference.

Susheela's parents had settled down on her mother's property after her father had retired. In a community where the practice of dowry was looked down upon, and where men were expected to make their fortunes independently, some of the General's contemporaries were a bit surprised that he had agreed to put down roots on his wife's property. Susheela herself felt that her father was not totally comfortable with the arrangement, but had acceded to his wife's wishes as it was the most practical option.

IV

When Joyappa awoke in the guest room of his in-laws' house, Susheela was getting ready for the evening. She had already bathed, and a cloud of some expensive perfume seemed to follow her around. As Joyappa headed for the bathroom, Susheela was sitting in front of a mirror, examining her face intently as she tweezed things, coated her face with powders and liquids, carefully applied something black in the vicinity of her eyes and put on her lipstick.

'You'd better hurry, Joy,' she said, still excited to be in her parents' home. '*After* you bathe,' she added pointedly, 'remember to wear a dark suit to dinner. Mummy's invited several interesting people to the party.'

'Okay.' said Joyappa, shortly. His spirits flagged. He had met many people Susheela considered 'interesting' and frankly, when they began to talk, Joyappa usually found it hard to stay awake.

Susheela looked especially pretty after her efforts. Still hurt from the cold reception by his in-laws, Joyappa's innate competitive spirit manifested itself. He decided that he, too, could look good when he tried. So he began by shaving carefully. However, after the shave, he still could see what appeared to be five o'clock shadow. So, he shaved carefully again, then rinsed and dried his face before evaluating himself. *Now*, he thought, *my skin looks as good as Susheela's.*

He showered and scrubbed himself thoroughly. The hot water on his pustules again gave him a lot of pleasure. He fought the urge to spend half an hour scalding his flea bites and switched to cold water, hoping it would cool his body sufficiently to keep from sweating through his suit later in the evening.

Joyappa towelled himself dry before dressing with extra care. His suit was new and tailored particularly well, accentuating his broad shoulders and concealing parts of his body that bulged in the wrong places. The tie was tasteful; his socks had a subtle pattern and matched his suit, while the black shoes were shined to a high gloss. The cologne he slapped on was understated and pleasing.

'My! You look nice,' said Susheela admiringly, as her husband put the finishing touches to his preparations by flicking some lint from his lapel.

'You don't look so bad yourself, Honeybunny,' said Joyappa confidently, as he looked his immaculately attired wife up and down. He took her by the arm and the fine-looking couple headed for the party.

V

While Joyappa and Susheela were getting ready for the evening, the guests had begun to arrive. Susheela's mother had invited the 'Who's Who' of the district to the party. In addition, there were prominent people from other states who had made the long and tiring journey for the famous war hero's anniversary.

A bar had been set up on the lawn. The night was clear and the moon cast its magical light upon the festivities. The pleasant scent of flowers wafted across the lawns. Several moonflowers had bloomed and their silvery glow added to the spectacle. If Joyappa knew anything about his mother-in-law, he was sure that she had planned every little detail so the garden was perfect for the occasion.

Susheela effusively greeted one of the beautiful people and Joyappa used the opportunity to gravitate towards the bar. He was served a fine Scotch whiskey that he sipped appreciatively before tuning in to an ongoing conversation. A wealthy planter was proclaiming that he habitually obtained a whopping two tons of clean coffee per acre thanks to his intensive cultivation methods and the tight, personal supervision of his workers. Joyappa doubted the veracity of the claim as he had heard that the man was a regular at the horse races in various parts of the country. Also, he was often found on the golf links, betting against his well-heeled pals. Joyappa decided to avoid the windbag and seek less boring company. He drained his whiskey and picked up another one from the friendly bartender.

Joyappa heard some talk about 'goals' and 'short corners' from a different cluster of people on the lawn. A tall, well-built fellow was talking authoritatively, while a number of guests stood around and listened with rapt attention. Upon questioning the bartender, Joyappa learned that the tall man was a former Olympic hockey player, so he drifted over to the group to listen.

Charmanna, the former Olympian, was saying, 'Oh, there was tremendous pressure. It seemed like the entire Dutch team was in our half of the ground, and you know our forwards were too lazy to play defence. Luckily, when the Dutch centre-forward collected the ball and feinted to the left, I wasn't fooled. I held my ground and sure enough, he cut back to the right, so I tackled him, dribbled past another player and scooped the ball to our centre-forward, who I had spotted unmarked at the half-line. He collected it cleanly and with the opposition pressing so hard, was able to score easily. The rest, as they say, is history.'

There was a chorus of praise from the admiring audience, for skill at hockey was a much valued commodity in the district. The former international player lapped it all up.

'Fantastic job, Charmanna,' said General Belliappa loudly, 'we're proud of you, young man—here, let me get you another drink.'

Joyappa hadn't realized that he had been standing just behind his father-in-law. Before he could slink away, the General turned around, and almost bumped into him.

Upon spotting his son-in-law, his expression changed so that a close observer, in better light, would have thought the General had inadvertently stepped on something unpleasant. 'Oh, it's you,' said the General, 'I didn't recognize you in a suit.'

Charmanna looked at Joyappa and burst out, 'Are you Joyappa, the hockey star?'

Joyappa was a little surprised and said, 'Well, I played a bit in college.'

'My God!' said Charmanna, 'Gentlemen, I played seven years of international hockey as a full-back and I can safely say that no player gave me as many nightmares as the man over here.

'Joyappa was unstoppable and our entire team quailed when we came up against his college. Believe me, this fellow should have played for India, and played for a long time.'

'Oh, I don't know about that,' said Joyappa modestly.

'Do you remember the game against our college when you scored a hat-trick?'

'Sorry. I don't remember the exact game,' said Joyappa, slightly embarrassed. He had been a battering ram of a centre-forward, who never paid any attention to the opposition, strategy or any of the finer points of the game. On many occasions, in his furious quest for goals, he had inadvertently collided with opposing defenders, some of whom had to be carried off the field on stretchers.

'See this,' said Charmanna pointing to his crooked nose, 'I tried to tackle you from the wrong side. You were so fast and powerful that when you changed directions, your shoulder hit me in the face and broke my nose.'

'Sorry, man,' said Joyappa, very embarrassed at this point. 'I didn't mean to disfigure you. I hope you're okay now,' he added lamely.

'I'm fine, now. It wasn't your fault, Joyappa. It was a privilege to be on the same field as you. I was so sorry to hear that you hurt your knee and had to quit the game. Do you mind if I shake your hand?'

'Sure, sure,' said Joyappa as he shook hands, somewhat self-consciously.

Taking all of this in was the General. Again, a close observer would have noticed a dramatic change in his expression. He looked at Joyappa, pride writ large on his face, and addressed his son-in-law, 'Hmm, I didn't know you were such a fine player. Well, son, let me get you some of that special Scotch that I picked up last year.'

One could have knocked Joyappa down with a sunbird feather. In all the years he'd been married, he was fairly sure that his father-in-law regarded him with all the affection he might confer upon a troublesome toe nail fungus. This sudden elevation into the realm of *Homo sapiens* was a hard adjustment to make.

The rest of the evening (at least, until dinner) passed in a pleasant, alcohol and praise-induced haze for Joyappa. His liquid diet was supplemented with lots of finger food including shrimp, grilled liver, barbecued pork and tender pieces of tandoori chicken. Many of the guests came up to him and made small talk. Our hero reveled in the attention and spoke authoritatively on a variety of subjects ranging from the use of synthetic versus natural turf for hockey to the Middle-East crisis. Fortunately, most of the other guests had also drunk 'a few too many' and didn't argue with some of his illogical views.

VI

The dinner gong rang and the guests, after a good deal of coaxing, finished their drinks and headed to the large dining room. The enormous teak wood dining table was covered with a snowy white table cloth. The room had a number of vases with tastefully arranged cut flowers that added to the ambience.

Joyappa thought it was a bit pretentious that little cards bearing the names of the guests had been set by each place. However, he admitted that it beat having to mill around and wonder where one should sit down. He wasn't too pleased to note that Susheela's mother was just a couple of seats from him. His card was between that of a 'Dr Viswanath' and a 'Ms Jaji Achaiah', neither of whom he had met.

Joyappa first introduced himself to Dr Viswanath, a small, balding, bespectacled man seated to his right. When he was on the verge of asking the doctor for a solution to his flea-induced itching, Dr Viswanath began to tell him in a weird nasal accent that was part New England and part rural south India, 'I teach and do research in a university in the north-eastern United States. I've been working for years on the influence of telomeres on longevity. We have got some pretty exciting results of late. When I started my graduate research in the US, I was working on carbohydrate chemistry, but I'm really glad that I switched to DNA.'

Joyappa's eyes glazed over. He understood little of what Dr Viswanath said and was puzzled about the reference to DNA. He thought DNA was the abbreviation for a statement he often heard from his wife—*Do Not Argue*!

Joyappa decided that he would talk to the person on his left. Jaji Achaiah was a young model and beauty queen who was now hoping to make it big in the movies. Before dinner, Joyappa noticed that several of the men had been hovering around someone in another part of the garden. The someone in question was Ms Achaiah. Joyappa could instantly see why she had attracted all that male attention. The young lady was willowy and filled out her diaphanous dress quite impressively. When he spoke to Jaji, he was pleased to find that she was amiable and didn't seem to have any airs about her.

The meal started with a green salad with French dressing. As Joyappa picked up his fork, he felt something rubbing gently against his left leg. He glanced towards Jaji who was nibbling at her salad. As Jaji turned and smiled at him pleasantly, Joyappa felt the rubbing increase in intensity.

Gosh! The sweet young thing is making a pass at me, thought Joyappa—partly horrified and partly flattered. He wasn't sure what to do. He almost choked on a mouthful of lettuce, but managed to control himself.

Unbeknownst to Joyappa, Jaji was quite innocent of inappropriate behaviour. The culprit was actually his mother-in-law's pride and joy—a Pomeranian by the name of Fluffy. Fluffy had escaped from her kennel and found her way under the table. The little dog liked Joyappa and rubbed against him in the hope of getting a snack. When Fluffy got no response, she nipped gently at Joyappa's shins. Joyappa turned red and quivered. Susheela's mother, noticing Joyappa's discomfiture and hoping that he would not ruin dinner, fixed him with a hard, unblinking look.

Joyappa tried to finish his salad. But, the friction against his leg had an unfortunate consequence. The pustules began to bother him again. The sensation was unbearable, yet he tried not to think about it. A little later, he again felt the gentle rubbing against his leg. He could not very well scratch himself. It would look odd, to say the least. If he *did* scratch himself, the chances of making contact with the attractive young woman's leg may be construed by her as encouragement. Joyappa groaned under his breath at the dilemma.

When Joyappa felt his inner thigh being rubbed, he decided *enough was enough*. She might have been Miss 'Something', and while he knew he looked good that evening—that certainly didn't give her any right to explore his nether regions. He picked up his salad fork and jabbed at the object rubbing against him. He thought he heard a yelp. He looked at Jaji and was surprised to see her still nibbling at her salad, quite unperturbed.

Joyappa was perplexed. His booze-befuddled mind, by a process of elimination, eventually led him to the shocking conclusion that it must be *Dr Viswanath* who was responsible for the inappropriate touching. He was well and truly horrified. He turned to his right expecting to see the scientist clutching his injured hand. To his surprise, Dr Viswanath was talking to the person seated opposite—a Brigadier with a military bearing and a big, bushy mustache. The Brigadier suppressed a yawn as he valiantly tried to follow the little scientist's animated description of how telomeres, which are found at the ends of chromosomes, affect the life span of all living creatures.

Before Joyappa could further investigate the source of the unwelcome contact with his legs, the impulse to scratch became so intense that his self-control broke down completely. The only thought on his mind was relief from the infernal itching— so fork in hand, Joyappa went to work. He scraped, prodded and dug at the irritated pustules on his shins. The relief was immediate. As he jerked his hand around under the table, Jaji assumed that he was indulging in some perverted activity and subtly moved her chair away. Susheela's mother's face turned dark like a thunder cloud, so Joyappa gave his legs one final scratch, and placed the fork by his plate. The tines were now speckled with blood from his efforts.

Dr Viswanath didn't seem to have noticed Joyappa's activities. The butler served the doctor the next course, which consisted of roast chicken and mashed potatoes. The absent-minded scientist said, 'Thank you. Thank you,' and picked up Joyappa's bloody fork. This was wrong on more than one level. Not only was the scientist guilty of poor etiquette in using a salad fork on the main course, but he was also using a heavily contaminated object to shovel food into himself.

Aghast, Joyappa watched the little man use the fork to transfer a generous amount of mashed potatoes to his mouth. He felt a bit guilty that he hadn't stopped Dr Viswanath. But what logical explanation could he have given the scientist? Joyappa sincerely hoped that the poor man's telomeres (wherever and whatever they might be) were not adversely affected by use of the bloody fork.

When Joyappa looked around to see if anyone had noticed the scientist's faux pas, he saw Fluffy near the door leading to the pantry. Fluffy had a sad and hurt look on her face as she stared at Joyappa. It was at this point that wheels began to slowly turn in his head and Joyappa realized that he had done a grave injustice not only to poor Fluffy by stabbing her, but also to his fellow diners by suspecting them of being underhanded in their conduct.

The rest of the meal was relatively uneventful. Joyappa found the fare bland, but that didn't stop him from putting it away. Before dessert, one of the General's colleagues from his regiment stood up and gave a speech. He praised the old warrior and mentioned some of Bellie's heroic acts that had become a part of regimental folklore. It was so moving that even Susheela's mother's eyes became slightly moist. Joyappa was impressed. He had not realized that his father-in-law was a brave and famous war hero.

The General, in a voice quivering with emotion, thanked everyone for coming. Finally, he said that he was glad that his daughter and the fine fellow she married had helped to make the occasion a grand success. Everyone applauded, Charmanna leading the way. Susheela and her mother were surprised to hear any public acknowledgement of Joyappa by the General. Jaji's perfectly plucked eyebrows rose in shock, since she had concluded that Joyappa was a pervert, but she kept her counsel.

Joyappa's heart swelled with pride at his father-in-law's words. His flea bites still bothered him, but he would worry about them later. He concluded that it was a grand party and the evening couldn't get much better.

VII

After dinner, in a move that was commonplace sixty years ago, but now might be considered politically incorrect, the General led the men to his study. The ladies were to be entertained by his wife and daughter. Some of the younger women, including Jaji, were outraged at the sexist practice, but didn't speak out for fear of spoiling their hosts' special day.

The walls of the study were panelled with dark purple rosewood and the floor was covered with polished planks of Burma teak. A few antique swords and firearms were mounted on the walls. Comfortable leather chairs were arranged around the room. A rare, original oil painting of Indian troops in action during World War I was displayed prominently on one of the walls.

This was a man's room. The feminine touch was obviously missing—and *that's* how the General wanted his sanctuary to remain. There were no silly romance novels in the library. Instead, the bookshelves had various leather-bound volumes pertaining to military history, unarmed combat, guerilla warfare, infantry and cavalry tactics, high-altitude warfare and assorted weapons. Not a single painting of flowers, fruits, landscapes, or adorable little children adorned the walls.

Upon entering the room, Joyappa immediately noticed a sideboard laden with fine liquors. General Belliappa motioned to Joyappa to help him serve drinks. Still glowing from the unaccustomed praise bestowed upon him at dinner, Joyappa gladly obliged. After all the men had been seated and served, Joyappa poured generous amounts of a very expensive French brandy into two glasses—one for the General and one for himself.

Joyappa watched curiously as the General closed and locked the heavy teak wood door to the room before pulling out a box of Cuban cigars that he'd hidden behind a book by someone named Sun Tzu. The General winked and smiled at his son-in-law, before offering his guests the cigars. Neither Susheela nor her mother would have condoned any kind of smoking—hence the secrecy on the General's part. Joyappa opened a couple of the windows to rid the room of cigar smoke, and the General smiled appreciatively at him.

General Belliappa seated himself behind his desk with a contented look on his face as he puffed away at his cigar between sips of brandy. Joyappa took the only vacant chair, and settled down to enjoy his alcohol and tobacco. Unfortunately for him, he found himself next to Dr Viswanath. Mercifully though, the scientist was talking to someone *else* about his research.

Dr Viswanath was explaining to a retired Colonel that his work focused on the causes of ageing and his attempts to delay the process. The Colonel gamely tried to understand, but was fighting a losing battle as Dr Viswanath spewed forth information about telomeres, telomerases, free radicals and something called apoptosis, which he explained was a form of cell death. Joyappa could see the poor Colonel had a glazed look on his face. About ten minutes later, the retired soldier concluded that being captured by enemy forces in his youth, and questioned by a hostile interrogator was more fun than his present situation.

Many of the men from the armed forces were discussing old battles, defence of the country's borders, arms deals and the bravery of the Indian foot soldier. Some of the retired military men lamented the fact that, unlike in the past, many youngsters from the district refused to consider the army as a career option.

Joyappa was content not to join in any of the conversations. He did, however, help himself to more brandy and cigars. He also made sure that the General's glass didn't run dry, and after each refill was rewarded with warm smiles from his co-conspirator. Joyappa was feeling a pleasant buzz, when things abruptly took a turn for the worse.

Dr Viswanath finished talking to the Colonel, turned his attention towards Joyappa and began to boast about papers he had published in world renowned journals. Joyappa groaned inwardly. He knew there was a good chance that he would wring the scientist's neck if he heard more scientific mumbo-jumbo. So he manufactured a deep, hacking cough to drown out Dr Viswanath's voice. Then, pretending that he needed fresh air, Joyappa finished his drink, adroitly pocketed a couple of cigars and left the room.

Dr Viswanath was disappointed, but not crushed. After all, getting federal funding from the National Science Foundation or the National Institute of Health in the US required a great deal of tenacity. Other than running experiments in his laboratory, the doctor liked nothing better than discussing his research. So, he ambled over to his host and began to talk to him. Exactly five minutes later, the General mumbled some excuse about his prostate, and quickly left the study.

VIII

Kannu and Susheela were still entertaining the women in the living room, so the General tiptoed past the open door and headed outdoors. He shook his head as if to clear it of Dr Viswanath's biochemical blather.

As he strolled past some rose bushes, he found himself in a corner of the grounds that he didn't normally visit. It was his wife's favourite part of the garden. In fact, the area housed several rare and exotic plants that Kannu had collected over the years. Each specimen was given much attention and care, and the results were plain to see. For three years running, Kannu had won the 'Best Garden' prize of the local horticultural society. The latest addition to the garden was a kidney-shaped pond that housed several unusual aquatic plants and different types of goldfish.

Kannu loved to sit by the pond and knit, read or just watch her fish. General Belliappa, on the other hand, stayed away from the area because he didn't want to listen to Kannu go on and on about her plants. He was also worried that he might accidently damage some rare orchid and have to face his wife's wrath. But most of all, he bore resentment towards this corner of her garden because Kannu lavished so much attention on her plants that *he* felt neglected.

As General Belliappa turned around to head back to the house, he spotted a red glow by the side of the pond. So he stopped and went towards the light to investigate. When he got closer, he saw his son-in-law seated by the pond, puffing away at a cigar. By his side, was Kannu's little dog, who was chewing on something as Joyappa scratched her under the chin.

'Well, son, what brings you here?' said the General.

'Oh, I'm really sorry I had to leave the room. I just couldn't take any more of that scientist fellow and his gobbledygook.'

'My sentiments, precisely,' said the General. 'That's why *I* bolted.'

Joyappa fished a cigar out of a pocket, lit it and offered it to the General. The General looked around apprehensively, before accepting it

'Oh, don't worry. No one will see us, the women are too busy exchanging gossip,' said Joyappa.

The two men sat in companionable silence. Joyappa blew smoke rings, but couldn't see the results in the darkness. He removed his shoes and socks and put his feet in the water. He found that the cool water soothed his flea bites. The General relaxed as he smoked and thought to himself, *Susheela's husband may not be the brightest fellow around, but he isn't such a bad chap after all.*

Fluffy stopped chewing whatever she was chewing and licked Joyappa's face. Joyappa scratched her belly for a while. He felt bad that he had mistaken Fluffy's affectionate rubbing against him during dinner for an inappropriate move by his fellow diners. Fluffy, in turn, seemed to have recovered from having been so rudely stabbed by Joyappa and had forgiven him.

Soon, the dog decided she needed more activity and jumped into the fish pond. She swam around for a while, but then got caught in some of the vegetation and couldn't get free. She thrashed around madly and began to yelp.

The General was horrified. What would happen to the

goldfish and the aquatic plants? Most importantly, what would Kannu say?

Joyappa's concern was for the little dog. He didn't want her to drown. So he quickly stripped to his underwear and jumped into the pond. In the process of untangling Fluffy from the vegetation, Kannu's carefully cultivated aquatic plants were ripped to shreds. Finally, Joyappa got Fluffy free and tossed her out of the water. By the time Joyappa pulled himself out of the pond, Fluffy had shaken the water off her coat and begun to sprint all over the carefully tended garden.

The General, who had never been shell-shocked on a battlefield, was paralyzed upon observing the mayhem. He finally whispered, 'Here, Fluffy. Come on, girl.' But Fluffy was so happy to be safe that she continued her mad run for a few more minutes. The path she followed was roughly circular and of her own making—she covered several laps at high speed in a counter-clockwise direction. With each lap she sprinted between the General's legs, around Joyappa, through several flower beds, and over a young cactus.

Joyappa, still in his underwear, tried to calm the little dog down. In the process, both Fluffy and Joyappa crushed some pansies, stomped on a couple of rare orchids, pulverized a few Lobster Claws, destroyed a Bird of Paradise and obliterated several *Hydrangeas*. Finally, Fluffy slowed down, launched herself into her saviour's arms and began to lick his face.

Fortunately, the General started to take charge as years of military training and combat experience came into play. He broke a branch from an ornamental palm tree, and swept the area in an attempt to cover both the human and animal tracks. Then, he asked Joyappa to keep the dog in his arms and walk towards the wall that encircled the compound. When Joyappa reached the wall, he was asked to turn around, take a large step to the side and walk towards the ruined garden.

General Belliappa restrained Fluffy for a few minutes as Joyappa put on his clothes and shoes. Joyappa started back to the house with a relaxed Fluffy in tow. The General followed them, but he walked backwards as he carefully swept away any evidence of their visit to the pond. Joyappa remained a bit puzzled at his father-in-law's strategy; so, in a low whisper, the General explained to Joyappa that Kannu would be very upset at the destruction of her precious garden. To shift the blame to some fictitious person, he had asked Joyappa to walk to and from the fish pond to create the appearance that an intruder had scaled the wall, taken a swim and stomped all over the garden before leaving by climbing back up the wall.

'I'm not the praying kind, son,' said General Belliappa. 'But, I sure as hell hope that your mother-in-law thinks someone else ruined her garden. Otherwise, we could be in serious trouble. Now, let's see the guests off.'

The General was right. If ever Kannu or Susheela were to find out who had destroyed the prize-winning garden, there would be hell to pay. Joyappa was very worried. However, both General Belliappa and Joyappa managed to put on a brave front as they wished the guests goodbye.

Jaji Achaiah thanked the hosts for inviting her to the party, but pointedly avoided looking at Joyappa. The last to leave was Dr Viswanath, who was explaining to Susheela and her mother about how he had used a certain chemical to prevent the shortening of telomeres of some poor lab animal. When the scientist finally drove off, everyone heaved a collective sigh of relief.

Later, as Susheela removed her earrings in their room, she said, 'That was a lot of fun, Joy. I think the party went swimmingly. Don't you?'

'Yes, Susheela. It did,' said Joyappa, a bit tentatively, wondering if Susheela suspected something about his antics with Fluffy in the garden. 'You know, I forgot to tell you that I have to be back home early to meet a labour contractor,' he continued, quite untruthfully. 'Maybe we can leave early tomorrow and get a bite on the way.'

'Okay, Joy. If it's that important, I could get ready,' said Susheela with mixed feelings. She was happy that Joyappa was showing some responsibility with regard to his work. At the same time, she would have liked to spend more time with her parents.

Much, much later, as the exhausted Joyappa drifted off to sleep, he remembered the enigmatic expression on the General's face. Before heading off to bed, the General had winked at his son-in-law conspiratorially and patted Fluffy on her head. Despite his slightly apprehensive look—possibly in anticipation of Kannu's reaction to the annihilation of her garden—Joyappa was puzzled to observe that the old man actually seemed to be quite pleased with himself.

IX

The next day, Joyappa was up early despite nursing a massive hangover. His mother-in-law had not surfaced yet, so Susheela wrote her a note explaining why they had to leave so soon. She was disappointed to hear from the cook that her father had left half an hour earlier for a game of golf. She would have liked to wish him goodbye in person. Joyappa, on the other hand, was filled with admiration at the old soldier's ability to side-step danger. All those years of guerilla warfare must have taught the General not to be at the wrong place at the wrong time.

As Joyappa placed the suitcases in the car, poor Fluffy made several desperate attempts to hop in, which were thwarted by Susheela. Joyappa felt bad for the little dog. But he didn't want to be around when his mother-in-law took her morning walk. As soon as Susheela was seated in the car, he gunned the engine and drove off.

Later that morning, at the Belliappa estate, a horrible, piercing wail cut through the silence of the morning as Kannu discovered the fate of her beloved garden. The traumatized gold fish that had survived the previous night's mayhem headed for cover at the very bottom of the pond, while the less fortunate ones floated belly up on the surface. Poor Fluffy hid under a bed and covered her face with her paws.

General Belliappa, who was putting for par on the rather tricky sixteenth hole of the local golf course, didn't hear his wife's anguished cry. He was quite pleased to sink the putt.

Joyappa was miles away and did not hear his mother-in-law wailing, either. He was enjoying a leisurely breakfast with Susheela in a new road-side café that served excellent idlis with mild coconut chutney, and freshly prepared Coorg coffee. As the caffeine cleared his fuzzy head, Joyappa thought back to the events of the previous evening. He smiled as he remembered the adventure and his narrow escape from disaster. Joyappa was glad that he was at a safe distance from his mother-in-law, although he sort of missed General Belliappa and Fluffy.

7

Joyappa Goes to the Dogs

I

Susheela was suffering from empty nest syndrome. Joyappa would not have used the term since he had never heard of the condition. But even *he* noticed that his wife wasn't her usual self. The children were back at their boarding schools after a long vacation. Their daughter had left a month ago as her school had re-opened a little earlier than Timmy's. It had been one week since Susheela and Joyappa had driven up to the Niligiris to drop their son at school. Parting had been painful as mother and son clung to each other and wept. Joyappa hoped that no one else had witnessed this display since Timmy was already a target for bullies. Joyappa tried desperately to disengage Timmy from his mother, but the boy had clung to Susheela like a hungry leech. Joyappa lost focus for a moment as he wondered if leeches became hungry or thirsty. Finally, he was successful at separating mother and child before leaving the sobbing boy in the care of his gruff, but fair, housemaster.

Susheela had cried during the journey down the steep, winding road to the plains. Concerned that she might suffer from dehydration, Joyappa tried to get her to drink some tender coconut water from a road-side vendor. Susheela mumbled something, shook her head in refusal and continued to sob. Joyappa shrugged before replenishing his own fluids with the water of two coconuts. He also slurped up the sweet, soft flesh inside.

An hour later, as they drove slowly through a game sanctuary, Susheela turned her face to her husband and said, 'Joy, I just hope our little baby will be okay. Maybe he won't get bullied as much this year.'

'I think he will be just fine,' said Joyappa. He wasn't being entirely truthful since he knew that Timmy was just the kind of nerdy kid who bullies love to target.

'Sometimes I wonder why we put the little darling in boarding school so far away.'

Joyappa decided that it would be prudent not to respond since it was *Susheela* who had insisted that their son be enrolled in the famous public school in the Nilgiris. In fact, Susheela had actually booked a seat for Timmy within a week of his birth. Joyappa suspected that it was a matter of prestige for her, since many of her friends had shipped their kids off to renowned schools located at various hill-stations across the country. As far as Joyappa was concerned, he would have been quite happy to have Timmy go to a local school. That way, he could have taught him the really important things in life—including how to shoot straight, play team sports and, of course, stand up to bullies.

When they finally reached home, Susheela headed straight for the bedroom and curled up in a foetal position on their bed, from where Joyappa periodically heard sniffing and sobbing sounds. Joyappa was concerned. He had never seen his wife in this state and was not sure what to do. So he chugged down a beer from his secret stash, watched a badly dubbed kung fu movie on TV and hoped his wife would be back to normal soon.

The next day started promisingly. Susheela was up early and had Joyappa's breakfast ready on time. As one would expect after her marathon weeping session, Susheela's face was a bit puffy and her eyes had turned red. There were also some significant behavioural changes that Joyappa was able to observe.

Normally, Susheela had little time for the cats. She usually tolerated Bug and Tiny, but often complained about how they shed their fur or damaged the upholstery. So, after breakfast, Joyappa was surprised to see Susheela actually petting them. The cats were equally surprised. Soon, Susheela picked them up, hugged them, planted kisses on their stunned faces and began to coo to them. After their initial shock, the cats began to lap up the attention. Joyappa was puzzled, but decided to wait and watch before contacting the nearest psychiatrist.

II

A couple of days later, a stray dog made its way to the back of the house. He had a glossy, reddish-brown coat and a muscular body, and was a frequent visitor. Joyappa quite liked the dog since he was very well behaved. He never chased the cats or dug up the garden. Joyappa had periodically seen him looking for scraps of food in the pit where the kitchen waste was dumped. After eating what he could find in the pit, the dog would lie out in the sun without bothering any one.

In the past, Susheela would shoo the dog away or ask Joyappa to run him off their property. So Joyappa would often yell at him half-heartedly and the dog would run away, circle the house and find a new place in the garden to sleep.

This time, however, Susheela's response upon seeing the stray was quite different. Joyappa was finishing his lunch as Susheela picked listlessly at a bowl of salad and gazed out of the window. Suddenly, Susheela's face lit up and she charged towards the kitchen. Joyappa, who had been monitoring his wife's strange behaviour since her traumatic parting from Timmy, decided to follow her. In the kitchen, Joyappa saw Susheela filling an enamel bowl with rice, mutton chops and a boiled egg. The chops looked good, and Joyappa wished they had been part of his lunch.

Susheela stepped out of the house and went towards the dog, saying, 'Here, fellow. I've got some nice chopsy-wopsy for you, boy.'

The dog bared his teeth and backed away, as all Susheela had done in the past was yell at him. So he couldn't quite understand the sudden change in her behaviour. Neither, for that matter, could Joyappa.

'Here you go, you poor, hungry-wungry fellow,' persisted Susheela.

The confused dog wasn't sure how to respond, so his upper lip contorted itself into an odd, Elvis-like snarl. Finally, he just put his tail between his legs and bolted.

'Oh, the little baby must be famished,' said Susheela, as she set the bowl on the ground and went back in to the house.

Looking at the nice chops in the dish, Joyappa briefly considered filching a few for himself. But he wasn't sure how

Susheela would react in her present state, so he went back to the excitement of the rice and curds on his plate.

A few minutes later, Susheela said, 'Oh, good! The poor baby's back.'

And sure enough, Joyappa and Susheela could see the dog happily wolfing down the food. As the last of the chops disappeared, Joyappa felt a sense of loss. But the dog looked so pleased with his meal that Joyappa didn't begrudge him the food.

Susheela was actually smiling as she said, 'I'm going to call him Darcy.'

Joyappa rolled his eyes. He was pretty sure that neither he, nor the domestic help would remember the name. In fact, he didn't think the poor dog would appreciate a name like that. Joyappa decided to just call the stray, 'Red Dog'.

Susheela began to feed the dog every day. He waited for his food, but never allowed anyone to get within touching distance. A week later, Red Dog brought a friend of his along. She was a thin dog with black and white fur and a fine, bushy tail. Susheela began to feed her as well, and named her Elizabeth. Again, Joyappa decided that the name was unsuitable and began to call her 'Black and White Dog'. Whereas the name didn't exactly roll off the tongue, there was no disputing that Joyappa's system of nomenclature had its advantages.

A grizzled brown suitor of Black and White Dog also began to hang around the house and Susheela happily fed him too. She named him Raymond—a name modified by Joyappa to 'Straymond'. Soon Black and White Dog began to bring two of her puppies along during her visits. The two pups were almost identical in appearance. Susheela named one, a greyish-black female with an inscrutable look, 'Sphinx'—Joyappa referred to her (the dog, that is) as, 'Sphincter'. Sphincter's sister had two white dots on her forehead. Joyappa took to calling her 'Colon', and was quite proud of his cleverness. Unfortunately, Colon stopped visiting a couple of weeks later. Joyappa hoped that no harm had come to her and she had found a good home.

For whatever reason, the dogs tended to respond to the names coined by Joyappa. Susheela was extremely frustrated that all of the dogs gave her blank looks and didn't respond to the names she had so carefully chosen. She angrily told Joyappa that he was stepping on her turf and taking over her pets. Joyappa just shrugged and, wisely, did not reply. The truth of the matter was that he could not remember most of the names that Susheela seemed to have pulled out of her Victorian novels.

Predictably, Black and White Dog littered a few months later and the canine population around the house increased. Soon, Sphincter also had some puppies. Susheela fed them all.

Previously, Joyappa had often hinted that a dog or two might be nice to have around. Over the years, Susheela had shown no interest in acquiring any more pets. She felt dogs would make a mess of her garden and house. In fact, she barely tolerated the cats. But now, there was a definite change in her attitude. This transformation coincided with Timmy's term at boarding school. However, it was well beyond Joyappa's realm of expertise to determine what biochemical changes had induced Susheela's sudden desire to acquire and nurture animals.

Joyappa managed to find good homes for some of the puppies, but several were retained—mostly females, as they were not in demand. Realising that any attempts to address the dogs with names of her choice would be futile, Susheela didn't argue when Joyappa named them Brown Dog, White Dog, Black Puppy and Jumping Bean. With all the meat and packaged dog food he was asked to buy for the pets, Joyappa found he was now very popular with the butcher and the local grocer.

In order to protect the garden and keep the four youngest puppies from straying, Joyappa employed several local masons and carpenters to construct dog houses and enclosures. However, he was unable to get any of the other dogs to stay in the newly constructed structures as they were too accustomed to running free.

III

Every time a dog disappeared for a while, Susheela would fret. Joyappa also found himself worrying about them, as the hazards they faced were numerous. Red Dog vanished for a couple of days. When he returned, Susheela observed that he seemed to have a constriction around his torso. Both Susheela and Joyappa tried to examine him when he came for his meals but Red Dog's reluctance to be touched by humans remained strong, and they could not determine what ailed him.

A couple of weeks later, Susheela noticed that wherever Red Dog slept in the garden, he left a wet patch on the ground. So, the next time the injured dog went to sleep in his favourite place under the shade of a jasmine shrub, Susheela managed to get within a few feet of him. She was horrified to observe that a thin wire had worked its way into the dog's flesh, thereby causing a foul-smelling discharge.

Red Dog had gotten trapped in a snare while visiting one of his girlfriends on a neighbouring estate. How he managed to get away remained a mystery since the wire was extremely strong. The setting of such snares was illegal, although many people used the method to capture rabbits and wild boars for food. It was clear to Susheela that the wire would have to be removed from Red Dog's body or he would die a painful death. So she quietly returned home and asked Joyappa to somehow extract the wire that was eating into the poor dog's flesh.

Joyappa approached the sleeping dog carefully from behind. When just a few feet away from his target, he happened to step on a twig. Red Dog woke up, suddenly saw Joyappa brandishing his wire cutter, and was away in a flash leaving a damp, malodorous patch on the ground. Joyappa was irritated with himself, and swore that he would remove the wire from Red Dog's body, come hell or high water.

Joyappa's second, third, fourth and fifth attempts to help Red Dog were unsuccessful. He would hide within the jasmine bush under which Red Dog usually rested after his morning meal. The dog was injured, but his vision, sense of smell and hearing were just fine. Joyappa's attempts at concealment were so obvious that Red Dog changed his sleeping place to a *Poinsettia* bush on the opposite side of the garden.

Joyappa's next attempt to remove the wire from Red Dog's body called for a more elaborate plan. He had just watched an action movie in which the majority of mindless violence occurred in a tropical rainforest. He was unsure about whether the rainforest was in Africa, South America or Asia, and didn't really care. The movie had a weak plot, but Joyappa liked it anyway. This was the part of the story that prompted Joyappa's subsequent actions:

A gang of thieves had stolen jewelry from the home of a millionaire. Upon setting eyes on the millionaire's daughter, one of the thieves had kidnapped her. The gang had evaded the police and escaped into the jungle. But they hadn't eluded Clint Newton, Private Investigator, who had been hired by the millionaire to recover his daughter and the jewels.

As the gang set up camp that evening, their hostage lay bound and gagged nearby. The leader of the gang, an unsavoury character with a scarred face, approached the young woman, removed her gag and untied her. The young woman sat up and massaged her wrists to get the circulation going. Another man approached the hostage, handed her a plate of food, said something crude and leered at her. Clint, who was watching from behind a tree, could not hear what the man said, but the young woman's eyes rolled in fear and her bosom heaved. It was the sort of movement (and bosom) that the eagle-eyed Clint didn't miss.

The leader of the gang walked over to the man and said, 'Stay away from her, Billy. Let's keep her safe until we get the ransom from her rich daddy. There's gonna be plenty of time to have us some fun after we get the dough.'

'Oh, okay, Boss. Boy, I just can't wait to get my share of the loot and have some fun!' said Billy with a crude smile, before he threw some wood on the fire. As the men began to drink, and the evening shadows lengthened, Clint knew that despite the leader's warning, he would have to act soon to save the honour of the young woman.

Clint waited until the men fell asleep and began to snore. Billy, who was first up for guard duty, was struggling to stay awake as he had drunk too much whiskey. The flames from the campfire died down gradually until just a few embers were burning. When Clint saw Billy nod off, he made his move.

Clint cut down some sort of flowering shrub and proceeded to hide within its foliage. Very carefully, the bush containing Clint moved into the clearing. There were several tense moments, but Clint managed to make his way to where he had seen the leader of the gang place a leather bag containing the stolen jewels. Miraculously, no one observed the strange moving bush as it approached the bag. Clint extended an arm, removed the jewels and filled the bag with rocks. Next, the bush made its way towards the young woman, whom it engulfed before slowly entering the thick jungle surrounding the clearing.

Joyappa was impressed that Clint Newton had so cleverly rescued the damsel in distress along with the stolen jewels. He would have been even more impressed if Clint had whacked Billy on his uncouth head, but he did realize that the young woman's safety was the detective's priority. At any rate, Joyappa decided to borrow Clint's ingenious technique to treat the injured dog.

After ensuring that Red Dog was not in the vicinity, Joyappa cut several branches of a *Lantana* shrub with colourful flowers that was on the periphery of the garden. He didn't think that Susheela would mind. He stored the branches in the shade and waited behind a tree for Red Dog to arrive. Red Dog appeared at the usual time, finished his meal, stretched, walked over to the middle of the lawn and settled down for a nap.

Joyappa waited for about five minutes to, some would say literally, put his 'plan in motion'. He stripped down to his underwear and smeared his body with diluted slurry of cow manure to mask any human odour (this particular plan was one that even detective Clint Newton hadn't considered). Using some twine, Joyappa then tied several of the smaller branches of the *Lantana* shrub to his back and legs. Next, he picked up the larger branches and covered the remaining 'bare' areas. Since his underwear didn't have pockets, he had to grasp his wire-cutters firmly between his teeth before beginning a slow, careful crawl towards his quarry.

Despite the elaborate plan, there were a few factors that Joyappa had not considered. The *Lantana* shrub had a lot of foliage, and there was no denying that its pink flowers were pretty. However, Joyappa realized very soon that the branches also bore a number of thorns that dug painfully into his flesh as he slowly moved towards Red Dog. Further, Joyappa suffered from an allergy at certain times of the year. This reaction was possibly due to the pollen of an as yet unidentified plant. Unfortunately for Joyappa, the allergy-inducing plant had flowered that morning and dispersed its pollen on the gentle breeze that wafted across the garden. His eyes and nose turned red and itchy. Yet, admirably, Joyappa continued with his approach towards his target with single-minded dedication.

Red Dog was now lying on his back with his eyes closed and legs in the air. Joyappa's plan seemed to be working. He was now within ten feet of the target. He took a deep, silent breath and gathered himself to pounce. In doing so, he inhaled a particularly large number of pollen grains that were on the verge of landing on a receptive stigma. Unfortunately for Joyappa, his sinuses betrayed him at that crucial moment. The sneeze exploded like a gunshot in a Spaghetti Western movie fractionally before Joyappa launched himself at his quarry. But Red Dog had had ample warning and quickly rolled over, hurdled a flower bed, and bounded away from the garden. Joyappa landed with a thud exactly where Red Dog had been lying. He was furious with himself and began to swear. He was so frustrated that he didn't care if Susheela or anyone else heard him as he raved and ranted and jumped up and down.

Finally, when he was exhausted and out of breath, Joyappa paused to wipe his itchy eyes and nose, and sneezed loudly. Suddenly, he felt that he was being observed. He turned around to find Susheela's parents watching him. Joyappa wasn't sure when they had driven up to the house and how much they had heard, but his humiliation was complete.

Susheela's father, Lt. General (retired) Belliappa, war hero and veteran of many battles, looked shell-shocked. He was struck by the resemblance between his son-in-law and a *Murrah* buffalo that had spent the day wallowing in a muddy pond.

Susheela's mother, Kannu, who was usually so proper and composed, stared at her son-in-law with her mouth agape. In fact, her lower jaw was so slack that a whole, unpeeled Coorg Mandarin orange could have been inserted comfortably into the vacant space.

'Oh! Hello, there,' said Joyappa, trying to sound cheerful, as he grabbed at a *Lantana* branch to cover his lower body, since his activities had dislodged much of the plant cover from his person.

For several days, Joyappa had been so intent on saving Red Dog that he had forgotten his in-laws had planned to visit that day. Susheela had been busy straightening the house in anticipation of the visit, and had not reminded him that morning.

The General was the first to recover. He tried to smile at his son-in-law, but failed.

Joyappa picked up another bit of foliage and attempted to cover his upper body. Then, trying to be a good host, he said,

'Please go in. Susheela's expecting you.'

Kannu, whose lower jaw, having valiantly fought gravity, had assumed its normal position, muttered, 'But, clearly, *you* were not.'

Just then, Susheela opened the front door and came out to greet her parents. She hugged her mother, but curiously found the sensation akin to embracing a large tuna in cold storage. There was no response from Kannu, whose attention appeared to be focused elsewhere. Susheela looked around and was shocked to see her semi-nude husband in the garden, coated with dark green slime, adorned by bits and pieces of a *Lantana* bush.

'Joy! What ...?' said Susheela, shocked at the sight. She felt totally mortified—her face became flushed and her perfectly plucked eyebrows shot up dramatically.

But she recovered quickly. She was, after all, the daughter of a warrior. Before ushering her parents into the house, she directed a glare of such venom at her husband that it should have left him terrified. But Joyappa was already sprinting for the back of the house and all Susheela could see was his rapidly disappearing back covered with flowers and leaves.

In the guest bedroom, Mrs Belliappa found her voice. 'Poor Susheela,' she said, 'Is that fellow quite sane? My God, I can't believe what we saw. I think we should take Susheela back with us. And the poor children—they *must* move in to our place.'

'Come, come, Kannu,' said General Belliappa. 'I'm sure there's some logical explanation for his behaviour,' although he didn't sound particularly convinced himself.

IV

Susheela's parents went to the sitting room after freshening up. The General had a couple of beers to take the edge off his shock, while Kannu and Susheela helped themselves to some homemade wine. Joyappa didn't appear for lunch, and Susheela, still irate, didn't bother to look for him. She had prepared a fine spread for her parents, who gradually relaxed and enjoyed the meal.

Meanwhile, Joyappa spent a long time showering as the gunk sticking to his body hair was hard to remove. He then disinfected the puncture wounds, scrapes and bruises incurred during his bungled endeavour. Later, he sneaked over to the back verandah and waited until Susheela and her parents retired for their afternoon naps. Joyappa attacked the leftovers in the kitchen with gusto, enjoying generous helpings of the pepper-fried chicken and biryani. The dessert, consisting of an excellent tart made of fresh mangoes topped with vanilla ice cream, also raised his spirits significantly.

Joyappa didn't feel like human company, so he set a comfortable chair on the back verandah and nodded off to sleep. Soon, White Dog hopped on his lap and Brown Dog, Jumping Bean and Black Puppy lay at his feet. As he napped, Joyappa dreamt of other strategies to trap Red Dog so he could administer the required medical treatment.

Later, Joyappa went for a long walk with the dogs as he wanted to give Susheela sufficient time to cool off. When he eventually entered the house, he found the General and Kannu were dressed for dinner.

By then, the General had recovered from the sight of his near naked son-in-law jumping around and screaming. He also remembered that Joyappa and he had shared a secret adventure resulting in the destruction of Kannu's precious garden several weeks ago. So, he greeted him cordially, saying, 'Hello, boy. How are you?'

'Fine, fine,' said Joyappa, not feeling particularly eloquent under the icy glare of his mother-in-law. He offered his in-laws a drink. Kannu declined with a shake of her head, so Joyappa poured a couple of large pegs of Scotch whiskey for the General and himself. With his inhibitions lowered, Joyappa began to provide an explanation for the baffling scene his guests had witnessed earlier in the day.

The General followed the narrative closely. Half-way through Joyappa's description, Susheela entered the room. Out of the corner of his eye, Joyappa saw her blink repeatedly as she took a seat. The blinking, Joyappa knew from years of being blinked at, signified disapproval. Joyappa fought the urge to leave the room for more pleasant surroundings, but decided that it would be rude to leave before completing his explanation. As Joyappa unveiled his elaborate plan to help Red Dog, there was a perceptible change in Susheela's attitude. First, the high-frequency movement of the eyelids ceased. Then, her eyes softened and she actually poured him a second drink.

Joyappa finished his narrative. Sporting a faraway look, the General said, 'Not a bad attempt, son. Not bad at all. Coating yourself with that cow manure was creative, I'll admit. Messy, no doubt—but certainly an innovative approach.'

Susheela said, 'Oh, Joy. Did you hurt yourself?'

'Just a few bumps and bruises. Nothing serious,' said Joyappa bravely, although his body was stiff and the puncture wounds hurt terribly.

'I'll see to them later, Joy,' said Susheela, and Joyappa felt good that things appeared to be normal between them. 'We can talk to the vet and work on helping poor Darcy later.'

The General cleared his throat, took another swallow of whiskey and said, 'You know, son, camouflage is a great way to get close to your target. Why, I can remember one time, I covered myself with sand, stuck a few cactuses (or should I say cacti?) in my helmet and crawled along the desert towards the enemy. I took out a machine gun nest. Poor bastards didn't know what hit them. Lost a fellow officer, though. Good chap, from somewhere up north—sadly, he wasn't skilled at camouflage.'

Even Susheela's mother, who was devoted to her Pomeranian, Fluffy, seemed to understand why Joyappa was prancing about semi-nude in the garden earlier in the day. She actually directed a look at her son-in-law that was about 15 degrees Celsius (give or take two degrees) warmer than the freezing glare she had given him before his explanation.

With the uncomfortable events of the morning more or less laid to rest, dinner was a relatively pleasant meal. Kannu and Susheela discussed gardening, their involvement in social work and the children. General Belliappa, whose wife and daughter remained largely uninterested in his military exploits, was pleased to have a captive audience in the form of his son-in-law. The General's tongue had been loosened by whiskey and he proceeded to tell Joyappa in great detail about his extensive experience in guerilla warfare. The incidents he described involved the garroting, shooting, strangling, stabbing, drowning, bayoneting and blowing up of unsuspecting enemies. He was also kind enough to advise Joyappa about the best methods to avoid having such unspeakable horrors inflicted upon oneself by one's adversaries. It wasn't the kind of conversation that helped one's appetite, but as Joyappa had imbibed even more alcohol than General Belliappa, he registered little of what the General said and was able to do full justice to Susheela's excellent mutton chops and potatoes.

This congenial atmosphere prevailed for the rest of Susheela's parents' visit. Kannu continued to be somewhat reserved with Joyappa as she had a niggling suspicion that he was responsible for the destruction of her precious garden several weeks previously, although she lacked hard evidence against him. When his in-laws left the following morning, Joyappa thought that the quiver at the corners of Kannu's mouth after she had made eye contact may have been a brave and unusual attempt to smile at him.

V

Joyappa's mind was now occupied with finding a way to treat Red Dog before his condition deteriorated. Since the time or frequency of the injured dog's visits could not be predicted any longer, asking the busy, local veterinarian to treat him on the estate would not be feasible. Joyappa decided that he would try to tranquilize the dog himself and dress the wound. So he paid a visit to the vet and explained the situation. The doctor was initially reluctant to have an untrained person administer anesthetic to the dog. But when he realized that the options were limited, and the animal could meet an untimely end without treatment, he provided Joyappa with some sleeping tablets and an injectable anesthetic.

A couple of days later, as Joyappa reached for a ripe guava on a nearby tree, he spotted Red Dog slowly walking towards the house along the driveway. Joyappa rushed indoors and informed Susheela who quickly filled a bowl with mutton broth, to which she added a few choice cuts of meat. Joyappa hurriedly powdered several sleeping tablets, stirred them into the broth and placed them under the shrub where the dog usually took a nap.

As Joyappa and Susheela anxiously watched from the kitchen window, Red Dog walked up to the bowl and sniffed at its contents. He looked around suspiciously, and without even tasting the broth, just laid in the shade.

'He can probably smell the sedative,' whispered Susheela accusingly, 'You must have put in too much of it.'

'If I had put in less, he probably won't fall asleep even if he eats the stuff,' said Joyappa, slightly hurt at the accusation.

Just then, Red Dog, who must have been very hungry, started to lap up the broth despite its altered flavour. He soon polished off the contents, yawned, looked around goofily and nodded off to sleep.

Joyappa waited for a few minutes before he sneaked up to the drugged dog from behind and quickly injected him with the prescribed anesthetic. The dog yelped in alarm and tried to run away, but the combination of sleeping pills and the anesthetic proved to be too much for him. His limbs seemed to lose co-ordination and he began to stumble around like some of Joyappa's inebriated friends. Before he lost consciousness, the dog threw up his meal. Joyappa was not alarmed as the vet had predicted this sort of a reaction when he handed over the medicines.

Susheela was horrified to see that the wire from the snare was lodged inside the dog's flesh. As Joyappa began to cut and remove the wire from the oozing wound, Susheela felt faint and almost blacked out. Joyappa cleaned and disinfected the wound, following which he carried Red Dog to the garden shed.

Susheela petted the unconscious dog and said, 'Oh, Darcy! Poor baby, I'll make sure you get all better.' After she had gently brushed his fur and clipped his nails, she began to kiss him. Joyappa had a flashback to the scene he had witnessed when Susheela parted from Timmy. He left the shed for a few minutes to maintain his sanity.

As Red Dog gradually regained consciousness, he began to get alarmed at the unfamiliar surroundings and the humans in close proximity, so Joyappa and Susheela left the room for a while. Later on, when they were certain he had all his faculties about him, they returned to the shed and released their patient into the garden.

When Red Dog trotted away with his tail held high, his pal, Sphincter, burst out from under a bush where she was hiding and, whimpering with joy, licked him all over his face. Both Joyappa and Susheela felt a great deal of satisfaction after their successful operation.

Susheela wiped a tear from her eye, took Joyappa's hand and said, 'Oh, Joy. I'm *so* proud of you. You saved my little baby.'

In a moment of weakness, Susheela added, 'Let's go in, Honey. I'll get you a piece of Lemon Drizzle cake that I baked for Asha. It will go well with your tea.'

'Sounds good, Susheela,' said Joyappa happily, as he silently thanked Red Dog for his good fortune.

VI

Unfortunately, Red Dog was highly accident prone. Whereas he didn't want to be touched by humans, he did not harbour similar sentiments about dogs, since he began to visit his many local female friends within a few days. Thankfully, he was careful to avoid getting caught in any more snares. However, on one occasion, Susheela heard the sound of fierce growling and some yelping several hundred feet from the house. Before she could investigate further, Red Dog appeared at the back of the house limping badly. He was panting heavily and his right foreleg seemed to have been severely bitten during a fight with his competitors. He looked to be in considerable pain. After drinking a little milk that Susheela put out for him, the dog vanished for a couple of days.

When Red Dog returned, Joyappa and Susheela were greatly relieved. He was still limping and Joyappa guessed that he would be permanently crippled. Red Dog spent most of the next two days around the house, eating and resting before taking off on another amorous excursion.

When the dog showed up a week later, he had obviously been in *yet* another fight and lost badly. The fur near his neck was dark from coagulated blood. Clearly, he was not a great fighter. He allowed Susheela to get close enough to take food out of her hand, but true to form, any move to pet or examine him was met with bared teeth.

Joyappa suggested that given his tendency to get hurt during his visits to various girlfriends, neutering Red Dog might be the best option to keep him healthy. Susheela wouldn't hear of it for the dog, but she did get a pleased, far-away look in her eye for a moment that scared Joyappa.

'How can you suggest something so inhumane, Joy?' she asked. 'Put yourself in his place. Would *you* like someone to do that to you?'

Joyappa thought to himself that even if it was not physically obvious, after several years of marriage, it did feel like 'someone had done that' to him. Wisely, he bit back his answer in the interests of marital harmony.

A day later, Susheela left for Darjeeling where she planned to attend a wedding and do a bit of sightseeing. Joyappa was now solely responsible for Red Dog's welfare. When he set a bowl of food before the dog, Joyappa was horrified to notice a moving white mass in the wound, along with the odour of putrefaction. Closer observation revealed that the white mass consisted of numerous maggots. The infestation was so bad that Joyappa was sure the dog would not survive without treatment.

Joyappa had the routine down. He resorted to his earlier method by grinding a couple of sleeping tablets and mixing the resulting powder with Red Dog's milk. After drinking the spiked milk, the dog went to sleep beneath his favourite jasmine bush. Joyappa sneaked up behind him and knocked him out with an injection to his thigh. When Joyappa took a close look at the wound, he gagged. The maggots had burrowed deep into the neck and created a network of tunnels in the dog's flesh. Joyappa and a couple of workers tried to pick the maggots out by hand, but there were so many that it appeared to be pointless. One of the workers suggested application of camphor would draw out the maggots. Magically, after sprinkling some powdered camphor on the wound, many of the maggots came out through the various holes they had made in the flesh. Yet, not all of them exited the wound. Since Joyappa had reservations about the effect of additional camphor on the dog's tissues, he knew that professional treatment was essential. So he loaded the still unconscious dog in his jeep and drove an hour to the nearest competent vet.

The doctor cleaned out the wound, pumped the dog full of antibiotics and inoculated him against various diseases. Following the treatment, Joyappa drove back from the clinic rapidly knowing full well that it would be difficult to control Red Dog if he regained consciousness in the vehicle.

Red Dog was then placed in the garden shed. Upon waking up, he wasn't happy about being prevented from being out in the open with his friends. When Joyappa tried to apply some medicine to his neck the following day, the patient growled. So he was forced to sprinkle the antibiotic powder on the wound from a safe distance.

Over the next week, Red Dog remained in the shed as Joyappa monitored his progress. Physically, he was such a wreck that, except for occasionally whining when other dogs were in the vicinity, he did not make too much of a fuss despite being restricted to the shed. Gradually the good food and antibiotics had him on the road to recovery. When he started to feel better, he began to get restless and attempted to break out. Joyappa realized that given his tendency to get injured, freedom for Red Dog would likely be the end of him. So, Joyappa took a bold, unilateral decision to ensure the dog's survival.

Joyappa knocked Red Dog out with yet another injection, hoping that repeated doses of anesthesia would have no adverse effects, and drove him to the veterinary clinic. The doctor was pleased that the wounds were healing well. Upon Joyappa's request, the vet made sure that Red Dog was well and truly 'fixed' so he would not be siring any more puppies. Joyappa had mixed emotions about his decision, but concluded that the somewhat drastic measure would greatly improve the dog's well-being. Given that Susheela had been staunchly against his plan, Joyappa pushed the niggling doubts about his own welfare to the back of his mind.

Following the vet's ministrations, the still unconscious dog was driven back to the estate. A couple of days later, Joyappa released Red Dog from the shed. His pals, Sphincter, Black and White Dog and Straymond were thrilled to see him. They greeted him by barking loudly, sprinting around the garden and licking his face.

Red Dog was also happy to be free. He certainly wasn't going to be winning any dog shows as he walked with a limp from his improperly healed foreleg, and his coat was still furrowed from the unfortunate encounter with the snare. Also, his right eye had turned opaque and sightless, possibly due to severity of the infestation by maggots. Yet, Joyappa experienced a warm, fuzzy feeling as he watched his patient being mobbed by the other dogs.

When Susheela returned from her visit to the northern mountains, she immediately looked around the garden for Red Dog. Pleased to find him in his usual place under the jasmine bush, she smiled and said, 'Hello, little baby-waby. Did you miss me?'

Red Dog was happy to see Susheela. He wagged his tail and barked a greeting. But when she tried to pet him, he backed away as usual to avoid physical contact. While Susheela watched him hobble toward a nearby *Poinsettia*, her eyes moist with emotion, she thought the dog looked a little different from behind—but wasn't sure just why this was so. She guessed that he had probably lost some weight.

'Poor baby,' she said, as she dabbed at her eyes. 'Don't you worry, Mummy's back home to take care of you and fatten you up, my little pumpkin-wumpkin.'

It was only then that Susheela observed her husband, who was standing in the garden hoping to be noticed. She addressed him as her attention quickly shifted back to the dog, 'Oh, Joy. Would you carry my bags in from the car? I've got some special treats for the poor baby.'

Joyappa didn't react right away as he was torn between feeling offended at Susheela's indifferent greeting, and hoping that her tears would obscure recent changes in the dog's anatomy.

'Come on, Joy! Hurry up! You really need to be on the ball,' said Susheela, impatiently.

'Oh, you have *no* idea,' muttered Joyappa to himself, as he hauled Susheela's luggage indoors.

8

Joy Hosts an American

I

It had been brutally hot and dry from the beginning of the year. The economy of the little district of Coorg hinged on the production of coffee and black pepper. The blossom showers, which are so vital for the induction of flowering of the coffee bushes in February or March, had failed miserably. Further, the previous year's monsoon had deposited a mere third of the usual precipitation upon the little district.

Borewells had run dry. Rivers and streams had slowed down to mere trickles, and the little rainwater stored in ponds and tanks had either evaporated, or soaked into the parched earth. Irrigation, therefore, was impossible for most of the coffee growers.

There were portions of Joyappa's estate where well-established coffee plants had wilted or were scorched. Many of the younger, less hardy plants had died. Several pepper vines were withering on the trees that supported them. The mandarin orange trees looked healthy enough, but hadn't received sufficient moisture to bloom.

Joyappa was not particularly bothered. For one thing, he decided that there was no point worrying about events beyond his control. Also, his ability to estimate the following year's crop was so poor that he didn't realize he was destined to harvest only a quarter of his usual produce. Frankly, Joyappa was getting a bit sick of the negativity and the all pervasive feeling of gloom that enveloped the planters and traders in the district.

At lunch, on yet another hot and dry day, Susheela had a request for Joyappa. First, she softened him up with a generous helping of meatballs in gravy. The unexpected bonanza stimulated Joyappa's appetite so he put away a mountain of rice with the meatballs. Dessert consisted of a rich chocolate custard. Susheela, who was normally so particular about every calorie that Joyappa consumed, actually served him a second helping with a smile. The dessert tasted so good that Joyappa forgot to ask Susheela what the dish was called.

'Oh, Joooy,' cooed Susheela, after she had waited patiently for him to finish his dessert, 'we'll probably have a house guest next week. I hope you don't mind.'

Joyappa loathed having Susheela's friends stay over. These 'house guests' were usually her snooty pals from school or college. He disliked having to be on his best behaviour. He also hated feeling left out when Susheela and her friends giggled about some event from the past about which he knew nothing.

Since the good food had made Joyappa mellow, just as Susheela intended, he didn't grumble immediately. 'Who are we talking about?' he asked, warily.

'When I was in college, we had an exchange student from America. As I've told you before, Patty and I became good friends and we've stayed in touch ever since. About a month ago, she said that her husband might have to make a business trip to New Delhi. She hoped he would be able to spend some time with us instead of hitting all the usual tourist traps. So, I said we would be happy to host him.'

'Hmm, an American?' asked Joyappa, skeptically.

'I'll be busy with the women's self-help group meeting the day he arrives. So, I was hoping you'd be able to pick him up from the airport in Bangalore and bring him home.'

'How long will he be here?' asked Joyappa, as the good feelings from his meal threatened to evaporate.

'Maybe a week, or longer. You'll probably hit it off with him. Patty says he was a star sportsman in college—just like you, dear,' said Susheela, deciding that a little flattery could do no harm.

Joyappa puffed up his chest, stroked his mustache and nodded in a self-important sort of way. 'I suppose I could do it. Do you mind if I take Chomu and Charlie along?'

Susheela was horrified. She shuddered to think of the mischief and mayhem that the three friends would create if left unsupervised in the big city. Yet, she managed to smile disarmingly, 'Our guest will be new to the country, dear. You don't want him to feel uncomfortable around a number of strangers, do you? Maybe it will be best if you go alone.'

'Well, if you insist,' said Joyappa, quite disappointed that his pals wouldn't be on the trip. But he soon cheered up when he realized it might be nice to get away from the district and all the depressing discussions about how poor a crop one could expect for the following year. He just hoped the American would be a regular guy and not some stuck-up fellow who was no fun to be around.

'Thanks, Joy. You're such a sweety-pie,' said Susheela, as she planted a kiss on Joyappa's cheek. She was quite pleased with the success of her strategy. 'His name is Joseph Scurlock. I've never met him, but Patty refers to him as Joe.'

II

On the day of his departure for Bangalore, Susheela packed Joyappa's bags and gave him a reasonable amount of money for his expenses in the city. Joyappa looked at the cash like a hungry dog that had been fed only half his prescribed ration of meat. Joyappa knew that the money would be *adequate*, but it wasn't enough for him to *indulge* in the attractions of the big city. Susheela pretended not to notice her husband's obvious disappointment.

The wheels in Joyappa's head began to turn—but slowly, as one might expect. That year Joyappa had decided to lease out his black pepper crop to a contractor. The contractor deposited most of the money in Joyappa and Susheela's joint bank account. Unbeknownst to Susheela, a substantial amount of cash had also been handed over to Joyappa, who conveniently forgot to inform his wife about the payment. In anticipation of a moment like this, Joyappa had squirrelled the money away behind a loose brick in the wall of the garage. So he mumbled something about getting some additional engine oil for the journey and made his way to the garage. Once in the building, Joyappa swiftly located the loose brick and removed the cash, which he duly hid in his underwear.

'Drive carefully, Joy,' said Susheela. 'Make sure you bring Joe back safely.'

'Yup, I'll do that,' said Joyappa, eager to be on the road and even more eager to have some unsupervised fun in the city.

He slipped on a particularly dark pair of gold-rimmed sunglasses from his collection, waved to Susheela and drove slowly out of the driveway.

When Joyappa hit the main road, and was sure that Susheela could neither hear nor see him, he stepped on the gas and roared away. He turned on some music that his friend Charlie had put together for him. It was a very strange collection—but Joyappa really liked it. Mournful country songs were followed by Kannada hits from the '80s; testosterone-driven heavy metal screams preceded Hindi or Bengali devotional songs; opera followed Carnatic music; while rock and roll was interspersed with rap, hits from Hindi movies of the '70s and Christmas carols. To some extent, Joyappa's progress was determined by what emanated from the speakers. Heavy metal made him floor the accelerator, hymns caused him to slow down considerably and all other forms of music elicited varying speeds, depending on the beat.

Although Joyappa kept himself amused during the drive by singing along or playing the tabla on the steering wheel, by the time he negotiated the unruly city traffic and checked in to his hotel, he was completely wrung out. So he raided the mini-bar, wolfed down something greasy from room service and fell fast asleep.

Joyappa reached the airport a quarter of an hour before the plane was scheduled to arrive. He remembered that the person he was to pick up was a Joseph—but try as he might, he could not remember the last name, although he knew it started with 'S'. Unfortunately, Joyappa had forgotten to ask Susheela for a photograph of their guest and had no idea what he looked like. So, he decided to follow the lead of the various taxi drivers who were awaiting passengers they had never seen before. Joyappa borrowed a piece of paper and a red marker, wrote '**Jo S**' in bold letters and waited for the passengers of the New Delhi flight to disembark.

Joyappa elbowed his way to the front of the group of taxi drivers, hotel employees, relatives and friends waiting to meet the passengers. The smartly attired flight crew was first out of the gate. Joyappa's neck seemed to swivel on its own accord and he took a moment to admire the flight attendants. A few minutes later, when the passengers started to troop out of the terminal, Joyappa raised his sign and looked hopefully towards them. Many of the passengers waved as soon as they saw their near and dear ones and exchanged hugs and kisses. The business travellers were more restrained as they scanned the assorted signs, and signaled to the taxi drivers or hotel employees when they recognized their names on pieces of paper or little placards.

Joyappa's arms had begun to ache, but he continued to hold the sign aloft and look hopefully at the passengers. He really wished he'd asked Susheela for a photograph of her friend's husband. His mind began to wander. What if their guest were to get lost or get into the wrong taxi and get kidnapped, assaulted or worse? It wasn't something Susheela would forget *or* forgive. He began to get nervous and broke into a cold sweat. Joyappa thought that life in a cave in the Himalayas would be preferable to the consequences of losing Patty's husband. Then he wondered if wild boars existed in the Himalayas. And, if there *were* wild boars, was hunting permitted?

After several dozen passengers had walked by, and the ache in Joyappa's upraised arms was becoming intolerable, a tall figure with short spiked hair, attired in a black leather jacket and black jeans looked quizzically at Joyappa's sign.

Ah, he's finally found me, thought Joyappa. He smiled welcomingly and said, 'Hello!'

'Hi, I'm Jo Stevens,' said a high pitched voice.

Joyappa expected an American football player to be larger. He didn't know much about the sport, but he had occasionally watched huge, helmeted and padded players crashing into each other on TV. He also knew that there were players who started football games by kicking the ball from the center of the field, or scored field goals by kicking the ball between two vertical posts. This delicate guy was probably a kicker who was wasn't involved in tackling people, thought Joyappa.

Joyappa shook a surprisingly petite hand and said, 'I'm Joyappa. How was your flight?'

'A bit crowded, but not too bad, thanks. Boy, it's sweltering here.'

Joyappa wheeled the cart with bags towards the parking lot as his guest followed. It was still very hot and he could hear the zipper of the leather jacket being opened behind him.

'I wasn't really expecting anyone to meet me. Did the hotel send you?'

'No, no,' replied Joyappa, 'I just decided to pick you up since you don't know your way around. The hotel's quite nice; we should be quite comfortable there.'

'Now just hang on a second,' said the alarmed voice behind him. 'So you *don't* work for the hotel?'

Joyappa turned around. The leather jacket was open revealing a lacy tank top that barely covered some very generous curves.

'But, but–' stuttered Joyappa. He was thoroughly confused, and wasn't sure how to react.

Jo Stevens stopped abruptly. Her friends back home had warned her about such men, and she had read the travel advisory on her government's website. So, she certainly wasn't taking any chances with this particular creep. Jo grabbed the cart from Joyappa, whose bulging eyes and general immobility reminded her of a large, frozen fish.

'*Get lost, perv!*' screamed the young woman, before kneeing Joyappa where no man likes to be kneed, and running back to the safety of the airport.

Poor Joyappa gasped and doubled up in pain, but he was in a public place and didn't want to rub himself where it hurt. The pain was excruciating and in the midst of his suffering, he wondered what he had done to deserve this sort of punishment. He took a couple of deep breaths but still couldn't straighten his body.

Suddenly, Joyappa heard a deep voice saying, 'Wow! That was rough. You doin' okay, man?'

'Hmm,' squeaked Joyappa.

He felt a big hand on his shoulder directing him to a nearby plastic chair. The voice said, 'Why don't you sit down a minute?'

Grateful for the sympathy, Joyappa sat down and tried to breathe deeply. When his vision cleared, he saw that the person next to him was an enormous red-headed man. As the pain in his groin subsided, Joyappa stuck out his hand and said, 'Thanks a lot. That was really painful.'

'No problem. I just saw that woman knee you in the nuts. I don't know what you did to her, but believe me, I feel your pain. By the way, my name's Joseph Scurlock.'

Joe Scurlock! Now, Joyappa remembered the name of Patty's husband. It *wasn't* Jo Stevens. He'd found his man—or rather his man had found him. Joyappa beamed through his diminishing pain. At least Susheela would not put him through the wringer for losing their guest.

'Hi, I'm Joyappa and I can't tell you how happy I am to see you.'

'Joyappa! Susheela's husband! Pleased to meet you, man. I was a bit lost as I exited the airport and didn't see you there, since Patty said you'd be meeting me.'

The big man smiled as his massive paw engulfed Joyappa's hand and crushed it enthusiastically. Joyappa noticed that his face bore a pleasant, open expression and that he had a very light complexion with a large number of freckles to go with the red hair. Joe had deep-set blue eyes and a scar across his chin, and his neck was unusually thick and muscular.

Joyappa straightened himself with difficulty and said, 'I'm sorry, but there was a bit of a mix-up. I'll explain later. I think we'd better get going.'

'Sure,' said Joe and after picking up his bags, followed Joyappa, who was gingerly walking towards his car with his legs wide apart. Joyappa drove back to the hotel with some difficulty. Steering wasn't a problem, but for obvious reasons, braking and changing gears caused him to grimace and whimper.

Since it was late, Joyappa ordered sandwiches from room

service. Over dinner in his room, Joyappa explained why he'd been assaulted by the young woman at the airport. As they washed down their meal with a couple of beers, Joe shook his head sympathetically and said, somewhat untruthfully, 'It could have happened to anybody, Joy. Stuff like that probably happens all the time.'

'Yes, you're right,' said Joyappa, already feeling better upon hearing Joe's comforting words.

III

The following morning, Joyappa met Joe at the dining room of the hotel. Joyappa felt almost normal except for a slight throbbing in the nether regions. His eyes lit up when he saw the spread before him at the breakfast buffet. He hoped that Joe wouldn't cramp his style (as Susheela usually did) by talking about the sodium, cholesterol, triglyceride and sugar content of the food. He'd heard that Americans were very health conscious. But Joyappa's worries proved to be unfounded.

Joe rubbed his hands in anticipation and said, 'Looks good, Joy. Hey, I hope you don't mind being called Joy, man.'

'No, I don't mind, Joe. What kind of food would you like?'

'Well, I guess I'll follow your lead. Like I said, it all looks good.'

Pleased with Joe's response, Joyappa decided to start with western food, sample the north Indian stuff and finish with a south Indian flourish. The two men did a demolition job on scrambled eggs, omelettes, bacon, sausages, muffins, nans, idli-sambar, paper dosas, *kesari bath* and washed it all down with several mugs of strong coffee.

Joyappa leaned back in his chair and undid the top button

of his pants to allow his distended belly some freedom. He felt pleased on more than one level. It had been a wonderful breakfast, full of flavor and other good stuff, without a single spoonful of oat porridge. Also, Joe Scurlock seemed like a pretty nice fellow who had matched him bite for bite. In fact, Joe may have eaten a couple of idlis and muffins more than Joyappa.

'That was great, Joy,' said Joe as he drained his last mug of black coffee. 'I'm glad my wife didn't see me put that grub away. Patty's always on my case about my diet.'

'I know *exactly* what you mean, Joe,' said Joyappa.

Joyappa decided that he quite liked Joe. He was not uptight, stuffy or judgmental. He'd even helped Joyappa last evening without asking a single awkward question. Plus, he loved his food.

Since he'd deemed Joe's company suitable, Joyappa thought that another day of freedom might be nice, so he said, 'Susheela wanted me to take you home today, but if you're tired, maybe we can spend another night in the city. I could show you around.'

'Sure, sure. It's totally your call, Joy.'

Joyappa called Susheela and explained that as their guest was feeling extremely tired after a rough flight, he would bring him home the following day. Susheela sounded disappointed, but agreed that Joe's comfort was of paramount importance and he should not be subjected to a long, tiring car journey.

IV

Since Joe wanted to shop for gifts, Joyappa decided to drive him to a busy street in the heart of the city. The traffic was bad, with autorickshaws, small cars, mopeds, motorcycles, scooters, SUVs, and city buses honking aggressively and vying for space on the narrow roads. In addition, bicyclists, pedestrians and the occasional cow also fought their way through the chaotic traffic. After months of driving in rural areas, Joyappa found the drive on the city roads quite stressful. When he finally took his eyes off the road to see how Joe was faring, he saw that his passenger had turned even paler and his eyes were firmly shut as his big hands gripped the dashboard like huge vices. Every time a horn honked (and horns were constantly blaring) Joe would wince like he had been poked in the arm with a sharp pin.

Joyappa hoped breakfast hadn't made Joe sick. However, after he had parked a good half-kilometre from the shopping area, Joyappa was relieved to see that some colour had returned to Joe's face.

'How're you feeling?' asked Joyappa.

'Oh, pretty good,' lied Joe, who was actually terrified by the density of traffic, the cacophony of honking, several near collisions and the casual disregard for rules of the road.

Glad that Joe seemed to be better, Joyappa shoved his wallet in the front pocket of his jeans and said, 'We've got a fairly long walk. I suggest you keep your wallet and passport in the front pockets of your pants—got to watch out for pickpockets, especially in crowded areas.'

Joe's business meeting had occurred in the sterile environs of a five-star hotel in New Delhi. This was his first attempt at being a pedestrian in India.

Joyappa led the way through the bustling mass of humanity. The American's senses were immediately under assault with strange odours, unusual sounds, brilliant colours and the incredible number of people on the streets. Joe gravitated towards a wall as the area was not crowded. Joyappa quickly pulled him back, just as he was about to tread on something that would have forced him to discard his footwear forever, and explained why the locals avoided walking near walls.

After following Joyappa for a few minutes, Joe felt something scratching his thigh. Looking down, he saw a pretty young girl who was about nine years old, looking beseechingly at him with her mouth open and her hand gesturing for food. On the little girl's left hip, was perched a skinny, malnourished baby with scanty red-brown hair. Joe Scurlock was moved; he decided to give the kids a little money. Before he could pull out his wallet, however, Joyappa dropped a few coins in the little girl's outstretched hand, and whisked Joe away.

Soon, two crippled men (one lacking an arm, and the other a leg) and a perfectly healthy looking woman with a young child approached Joe in quick succession, hoping for alms. Joyappa gave each of them some money, followed by a bloodshot glare that sent them scurrying away to look for unaccompanied foreigners.

When Joyappa and Joe reached the busy street that constituted the main shopping area, Joe was astonished at the number of unprepossessing shops that lined the street and stocked their respective specialities. These businesses included leather goods sellers, sweet-meat stalls, carpet outlets, stationery shops, sports goods stores, cloth shops, hardware suppliers, shoe shops and handicraft outlets. The shops were miniscule in comparison with the superstores in his hometown, and could only accommodate a few customers at a time.

Since Joe wanted to purchase gifts for friends and family

back home, Joyappa helped him buy a few handmade carpets, intricately carved items of sandalwood and rosewood, and assorted handloom-woven fabrics. Guessing that the prices would be driven up for the foreign tourist, Joyappa drove a hard bargain. On a couple of occasions, Joyappa signaled to Joe and stormed out of a shop claiming prices were too high, only to have the shopkeeper follow them out and beg them to buy his wares at a hugely discounted rate. Joe found it quite remarkable that Joyappa's tactics had reduced prices to a mere quarter of what was originally quoted, but he wasn't complaining. The shopkeepers even made arrangements to ship the purchases to Joe's address in the midwestern United States, so he wouldn't have to haul them around.

As part of the cultural experience, Joyappa decided to treat Joe to some street food. Aware that Joe's stomach might not be able to tolerate anything that wasn't hygienically prepared, Joyappa chose a vendor he remembered from his college days in the city who had a reputation for cleanliness.

A four-wheeled cart with the legend, 'Simon's Snakks' was stationed at the end of the street. Simon was a large, dark person with a round face partially obscured by a massive upturned mustache. Remarkably, save for a few silver strands near his temples, Simon looked the same as he did when Joyappa was a student in the city. Simon was doing brisk business, so Joyappa and Joe got in line behind several other customers. When it was their turn to order, Simon's pleasant face broke into a huge smile as he recognized his old customer.

'Joyappa Saar, how are you?'

'Fine, Simon. How's business, and how are you?'

'Very good. Business also good. My son having another one

cart near City Market. Are you still playing hockey, Joyappa Saar?'

'No, Simon. I stopped playing after my knee injury.'

Simon was a big fan when Joyappa was a college hockey star and the toast of the town. In fact, Simon had made a fair amount of money by betting on Joyappa's team during various tournaments and city league matches.

Simon even remembered the match when Joyappa hurt his knee, and now looked a bit sad as he addressed Joe and said, 'Mister, Joyappa Saar was very good hockey player. I watched all his matches.'

'Hmm, is that right?' said Joe, looking very interested.

Simon's hungry customers who were still waiting in line began to get a little restless. Without asking Joyappa or Joe what they wanted, Simon piled assorted meats—some dark, some white and others flaming red in colour—on a piece of flatbread, before topping it off with a dark, viscous sauce.

'How much, Simon?' asked Joyappa, as he fumbled for his wallet.

'For champion like you—nothing,' replied Simon with a huge smile, and despite Joyappa's best efforts, absolutely refused to accept any money.

Joyappa and Joe found a place by the shade of a nearby building and proceeded to tuck into their lunch. The food was hot, and obviously spicier than Joe was used to, but he didn't complain and ate with gusto.

'That was great,' said Joe, even as the spices caused little beads of sweat to dot his forehead and nose.

Joyappa decided to get a couple of sweet lassis from 'Naga's Kool Bar' to settle their stomachs. Joe gulped down the cool, creamy drink, smacked his lips and said, 'Man, that was really good! Thanks, Joy.'

'Glad you liked it,' said Joyappa.

'So you were quite the hockey player, huh? I didn't even know you guys had ice rinks here.'

'Yes, I used to play a bit of hockey. Not *ice* hockey—we play field hockey in India.'

'Well, back in the States, I've only heard of women playing field hockey. So did you wear skirts when you played?'

Joyappa wasn't sure if Joe was being facetious, so he tersely said, 'No, we wore shorts.' He proceeded to explain the intricacies of the game to Joe, who seemed genuinely interested.

Joyappa wanted to pack in all the fun he could before heading back home, so he asked Joe if he would like to see a movie. Joe indicated he was game, so Joyappa decided that a Hindi movie would enhance his guest's cultural experience. So, off they went to a nearby multiplex to watch the latest blockbuster.

There were no subtitles, so Joe couldn't understand much of the dialogue. Since Joyappa's knowledge of Hindi was rudimentary, he barely understood the conversations, either. However, it was the kind of movie that wouldn't have made sense even if they were native Hindi speakers. There were fight scenes in the slums of an Indian city, car chases in the streets of San Francisco and sudden song and dance sequences in the Swiss Alps where pretty girls pranced around in the snow wearing scanty clothes. In the midst of all this frenetic activity, the leading man's parents disowned him for wanting to marry a young woman from an 'unsuitable' family. By the end of the movie, however, everyone had magically put their differences aside, so it all ended in a big, happy wedding in Sydney, Australia.

Critics had slammed the film, but Joyappa thoroughly enjoyed it. He hoped Joe had liked the movie, as well. As the credits began to roll, Joyappa became concerned when he saw Joe dabbing at his eyes and sniffing. He was relieved to hear the big fellow say, 'That was great, Joy. Sorry, I got a little emotional thinking of Patty and our wedding.'

Joyappa felt bad that he had upset his guest. He was a bit puzzled, because he didn't think there was anything in the movie to get emotional about. He decided to make amends by helping Joe to forget about Patty for a while. So, Joyappa led the way to his favourite watering hole in the city.

The *Happy Fun Bar* consisted of a shabby little room that most discerning people would classify as a 'dive'. There was a TV in the corner on which some long forgotten cricket match from the '80s was being replayed. Obviously, it was a match that India had won—or no one would have watched. The prices were reasonable and the liquor was not watered down. Men came here to drink. No fancy cocktails or mocktails adorned with tiny, colourful umbrellas were served here—just good, hard liquor that made people forget their problems for a while.

Joyappa ordered rum, while Joe opted for beer. Joe appeared to like the Indian brew and easily downed one bottle after another. Joyappa kept a close watch on his guest and was disappointed to see that Joe still looked a little morose. He eventually realized that given Joe's body weight, beer wasn't going to effect a change in his mood, so he tried to convince him about how wonderful the local rum tasted. With some coaxing, Joyappa managed to get Joe to try the cheap, strong liquor that he favoured. After a few stiff drinks, Joe's sad look faded away and his face assumed the expression of a boxer who'd been hit on the chin by a powerful uppercut. Joyappa plied him with more rum until he was sure that all sad thoughts were completely erased from Joe's mind.

It was fairly late when Joyappa and Joe finally left the bar, wobbled their way to the car, and drove back to the hotel. Fortunately, traffic had eased up a bit and Joyappa, despite violating the law by being 'under the influence', managed to get them back without any mishaps.

The potent mixture of beer followed by rum had made Joe uncommunicative. In fact, when Joyappa offered to order dinner, there was no response from Joe, whose glassy-eyed expression made Joyappa worry that he'd suffered lasting brain damage. Finally, Joe rested his head on a pillow, closed his eyes and went to sleep fully clothed. In the adjacent room, Joyappa (after making short work of two plates of rich chicken biryani) spent a restless night worrying about his guest and what Susheela might do if he had irreversibly harmed Joe.

Late the next morning, Joyappa looked pale and disheveled when he knocked on Joe's door. He was relieved when the door opened immediately to let him in. Joe looked terrible. His eyes were bloodshot and he was clutching his temples. Yet, he smiled and said, 'Hey, Joy. Come on in. It's been a while since I've been so badly hung-over. But, man, was that a *great* day—we gotta do it again sometime. Thanks, bud.'

Joyappa smiled. He decided that he really liked hosting

Joe. In fact, he wished he could get him to move to India. Life would certainly be more interesting.

'If you don't feel up to having breakfast now, I thought we could leave when you're ready and stop for a bite on the way home.'

'Sure. That works for me.'

V

Thanks to the previous night's drinking session, Joyappa and Joe ended up leaving Bangalore too late to avoid the worst of the traffic. The day was brutally hot and Joyappa had the air conditioner cranked up all the way. Both men wore very dark sunglasses. Mercifully, Joe fell asleep within five minutes of departure and missed the stressful drive to the outskirts of town. He awoke briefly as they passed some magnificent rock formations, but soon nodded off again. A little later, he woke up as they drove through some busy towns, but quickly shut his eyes as Joyappa negotiated his way past bullock carts on large wooden wheels, overloaded trucks, buses, pedestrians, stray dogs and assorted three and four-wheeled vehicles. When he opened his eyes again, they were driving past lush sugarcane and rice paddy fields.

Joyappa decided that Joe was looking tired, so he stopped by the side of the highway where a thin, sunburned man was selling tender coconuts to passing motorists. When they got out of the air conditioned vehicle, the heat from late morning sun felt like they'd stepped into a furnace.

Both men were sweating profusely. Joe, being unused to the tropical heat and still hung-over, looked pale and unsteady. Joyappa decided that his guest should have his fluids replenished.

He signaled to the coconut seller who was looking towards them expectantly. The man took the once-white cloth that was draped over his left shoulder and wrapped it around his head. He picked up a tender coconut, deftly sliced off the top with a knife, slipped in a plastic straw and handed it to Joe with a flourish, before doing the same for Joyappa. After they drank the coconut water, Joyappa decided that he'd better get more fluids into Joe.

The thin man was only too happy to supply additional coconuts, which were quickly drained by the travellers. Expertly wielding his knife, he fashioned broad 'spoons' from the sides of the coconuts, before splitting them in half. Joe observed the process with great interest. He then watched Joyappa scoop out and slurp up the sweet, white flesh and needed no urging to follow suit.

'Wow, that was refreshing, Joy,' said Joe. 'I'm feeling much better already.'

Thanks to the substantial fluid intake, and the lack of a restroom in the vicinity, Joyappa was forced to locate a suitable shrub off the highway. When he pointed to the base of a large tamarind tree, Joe was a little surprised, but soon followed Joyappa's example.

Later, Joe smiled and said, 'That was great, Joy. We'd have been arrested or fined if we did that in public back home. But I gotta say, some things feel better outdoors—just need to be careful about wind direction, huh?'

Joyappa was pleased that his guest seemed to be better when they resumed their journey. The traffic wasn't too heavy, so Joe felt a little more relaxed and was able to enjoy the scenery that was so very different from that of his hometown. He still winced every time a horn blared, and clutched at the dashboard at every close call; however, he seemed much less terrified than before. Seeing Joe's delicate state, Joyappa wisely decided not to play his eclectic collection of music on the homeward journey.

Joyappa later stopped at a restaurant along the highway and picked up some sandwiches and coffee. Joyappa ate as he drove and quite enjoyed the food. Joe, on the other hand, tried the sandwich and found that it smelled and tasted unlike any sandwich he had ever eaten. The soggy bread was coated with a thick spread redolent of stale masala that overpowered any other flavor the unidentified filling might have possessed. He briefly considered telling Joyappa that he just couldn't eat it, but realized that his host might get offended. So, when Joyappa slowed to shout at a pregnant, unmoving water buffalo blocking the road, Joe took the opportunity to discreetly toss the sandwich outside. As they squeezed past the animal, he hoped that the poor thing wouldn't eat the awful sandwich.

Fuelled by food and caffeine, Joyappa was motoring along briskly. In order to control speeding, several humps had been constructed on the highway at varying intervals. Since Joyappa could never remember where the poorly marked speed breakers were located, he hit most of them at high velocity, causing his dozing passenger to be woken violently. There is little doubt that anyone with a neck of normal dimensions would have suffered serious whiplash. Fortunately, Joe's neck was so thick and muscular that he escaped unscathed.

A few hours out of Bangalore, Joyappa's phone rang. It was Susheela, who wondered why they were not home yet.

'You know how bad rush hour traffic is, Susheela. We set

off late since Joe was tired after his flight,' said Joyappa, not being totally honest.

'Is that so?' said Susheela, skeptically. 'Drive carefully, Joy, and head straight home. I don't want you taking detours to places you shouldn't be taking our guest.'

Strong, dry winds had begun to blow across the road, causing tall coconut and arecanut trees in the fields to sway from side to side. Most drivers fought to stay in their lanes as powerful gusts of wind buffeted their cars. Joe's massive bulk, however, meant that Joyappa's vehicle was largely unaffected by such issues.

Joyappa drove through Srirangapatna. He wondered if Joe would be interested in the town's rich history. Then, he remembered Susheela's phone call and decided against stopping. As he pondered the merits of a quick trip through Mysore to show Joe the garden city's charms, his phone picked up a message from Susheela reminding him to make sure that he brought Joe home quickly and safely. It required great self-control for Joyappa to veer off in a south westerly direction that would take them home, and sadly, away from the attractions of the city.

Upon finally crossing the check post guarding the entrance to Coorg, Joyappa experienced the usual, comforting sensation that he was on home soil. Despite the uncharacteristically high temperature, he felt that Coorg was greener, and several degrees cooler, than the neighbouring districts.

The roads improved, so Joyappa drove rapidly. When they were about half a kilometre from his driveway, he shifted down and the speed dropped dramatically. Knowing that Susheela could be lurking anywhere, he used his turn signal for the first time in hours, sedately drove up to the house and parked beside the front door.

Joe woke up and looked around at the colourful garden, wondering for a moment where he was. Susheela, who was snipping off spent blooms from her plants, hurried towards the car with a bright smile.

After Joyappa performed the introductions, Susheela stuck out her hand and said, 'Hello, Joe. I am so glad you could come. I really wish you could have brought Patty with you.'

In that open, friendly way that is so typical of the residents of America's vast heartland, Joe shook hands with her and said, 'Pleased to meet you, Sue. I've heard so much about you. Thanks for having me over.'

'The pleasure is ours. How is dear Patty?'

'Good, good. Yeah, she's just great but she couldn't get away with me,' said Joe. Then he appeared to remember something and said, 'Dang! Before I forget, Patty asked me to give you a great big hug.'

Joe then proceeded to enfold Susheela in his massive arms. As Joe squeezed her enthusiastically, and inadvertently lifted her off the ground, Susheela was taken by surprise. She felt as helpless as a little fawn in the coils of a python. Seconds before she was danger of losing consciousness, the pressure eased and the big man put her down gently.

Susheela took a moment to catch her breath, before inviting Joe inside. She then called out to Joyappa, who was unloading the car, 'I thought you'd be here a couple of hours ago. Anyway, I hope you've been taking care of Joe properly.'

Joyappa pretended not to hear Susheela's comments as he hauled the bags in to the house. He fervently hoped that Joe would only provide a censored version of their activities, if asked. Since both Joyappa and Joe were tired, they went to bed soon after an early dinner. The cats, pleased to have Joyappa back, curled up on his chest and fell asleep.

VI

The next morning, Joe woke up feeling refreshed. Joyappa, although a bit sore from driving on bad roads, also was more relaxed. Susheela had already fed the animals and finished her breakfast. She greeted Joe warmly and poured him a glass of freshly squeezed juice.

'I hope you like papaya,' she said to Joe and placed large, boat-shaped pieces of the fruit before Joe and Joyappa.

'Can't say I've tried it before, Sue,' said Joe, politely. 'It sure looks good, though.'

Joyappa finished his fruit quickly, eagerly anticipating a breakfast consisting of eggs and interesting stuff including bacon, sausage and ham, in honour of their guest. However, when Susheela brought out two large bowls of steaming oat porridge, his face fell. Joyappa looked up to find his expression mirrored on Joe's face.

'But Sue, I'm not big on oatmeal. Can I get some eggs, instead?' asked Joe.

Joyappa looked on eagerly, hoping he'd also benefit from Joe's request. Before Susheela could respond, Joyappa quickly added, 'Yes, Susheela, I think you should serve some fried eggs with bacon instead of porridge.'

'You do, do you?' she said in a cold, cutting voice.

'Definitely,' said Joyappa, but his voice sounded far from forceful, even to his own ears.

'Let me tell you something, Joy. Your cholesterol levels are off the charts, you weigh too much unless you've grown about five inches taller since your last medical exam; and as for your Body Mass Index—the less said the better. So, I suggest you eat what is put in front of you, and not much else.'

Joyappa averted his eyes and proceeded to eat his porridge. He felt like a naughty boy in primary school, who had been ordered to bend over in front of the entire class (including girls), before being soundly caned on his tender rear end. The feeling was familiar, since he had 'been there and had that done to him' many years ago.

'But Sue, *I'm* in pretty good shape. A couple of eggs over easy, with some bacon, wouldn't hurt me,' said Joe with a smile.

Susheela smiled back sweetly, then blinked several times as she looked at Joe. Joyappa knew the warning signs—Joe, naturally, did not.

'Well, Joe, as you know, Patty and I go back a long way. We're constantly in touch via e-mail. Jet lag and the change in circadian rhythms have probably clouded your memory, so I will take this opportunity to remind you that you've been advised to reduce your consumption of red meat, eggs, whole milk, sodium, cheese and fried food. And remember, that list is not comprehensive.'

Susheela paused, blinked a few more times and continued, 'Patty has asked me to ensure that your diet, when you are with us, does not deviate from what you have been advised. So, Joe, I suggest that you eat up that porridge and forget about bacon and fried eggs. Or, would you rather have me call Patty on the speaker phone so that we could all hear what she has to say?'

'Ummmm. Naah, no need to do that, Sue. Actually, this oatmeal looks pretty good to me,' replied the big fellow, who was neither smiling nor feeling particularly big anymore.

'Jolly good,' said Susheela. She looked pleased as both men ate their porridge without further protest.

To cover their embarrassment, Joyappa asked Joe, 'So, I hear you were a good football player.'

'Yup. There's some real good high school football played where I grew up back in Ohio. I was recruited out of high school by several big-time colleges. Finally, chose to stay in the Midwest. What can I say? I got to play close to home on a full scholarship. Loved it, man.'

'You should tell me more about the game,' said Joyappa. 'I've watched a few Super Bowls on TV—looks interesting, but I don't know much about the rules.'

'Sure, Joy. I got a couple of games on disc, we can watch them sometime.'

When Susheela left the room to bring them some tea, Joe lowered his voice and continued with a wink, 'Girls, man, Joy— they loved hanging around football players. College was great. Mind you, classes and those stuffy professors were a drag, but the rest of it was fun.'

Joyappa nodded through a mouthful of coagulating porridge. He thought that Joe's evaluation of the academic part of college education was exactly right.

'I played linebacker in college. Defense, you know. I just loved the contact. It's just great to hit people, and, I gotta say, I creamed lots of guys.'

Joyappa looked at Joe's thick fingers, which were gripping the porridge spoon tightly and the intense glare as he thought of the offensive players he had tackled in college. Joyappa felt a twinge of pity for the opponents who had the misfortune of being 'creamed' by Joe.

'Then, junior year,' continued Joe in a more somber vein, 'we were unbeaten and playing for our conference championships— might have been over ninety thousand folks in the stands— when some cheap-shot artist from the other team hit me in the knee with his helmet. I heard something pop, it hurt like hell and I couldn't run anymore.'

Joyappa looked away. He felt Joe's pain.

'I could have been in the pros and made a lot of money. There were pro scouts and agents sniffing around for a couple of years. After I got hurt and had major surgery, my knee just wasn't the same. Those agents and scouts just vanished. Can't blame them, I guess. No point hanging around damaged goods,' concluded Joe, philosophically.

'That must have been hard,' said Joyappa, sympathetically.

'Yeah, that was a rough time, Joy. But you know how it goes. That guy who served us that grub in Bangalore said that you were one heck of a hockey player.'

Joyappa shrugged, a little sadly, 'Yes, I think I could have made a career out of it, but once I hurt my knee, I just couldn't do the same things on the field. Plus, I was needed to help out at home.'

In an attempt to lighten the atmosphere, Joe said, 'I guess you must have looked pretty good in a skirt, huh? I was wondering why you didn't play a real man's sport like football that has physical contact, instead of a girly sport, Joy?'

Joyappa was not amused. He tried to think of a suitable retort, but repartee wasn't his strong suit. So he finally said, quite honestly, 'When *I* played, it *was* a contact sport. It may not have been legal, but I banged into a lot of defenders. And, we wore shorts, *not* skirts. I'm proud to say that I got hit many times by sticks and hockey balls, and if you must know, it hurt like crazy. At least, *we* didn't play with helmets or armor or pads or whatever American football players wear to cover their delicate little bodies.'

Worried that he had offended Joyappa with his joke, Joe said, 'Hey, Joy. No offense. I was just kidding, bud.'

'Oh, I knew that,' said Joyappa with a smile. But the smile was forced, because Joe's words rankled.

VII

Joyappa hadn't seen his friends for a couple of days, and missed them. So he called Chomu and asked if he could meet in town. Chomu, who was perpetually lonely since his wife spent most of her time away from him, was only too keen to get together.

Joyappa lied to Susheela saying that he needed to pick up some pesticide for the estate. Normally, if Susheela knew that Joyappa was heading for town, she would insist that he shop for groceries. However, being a bit of a health nut, Susheela never asked Joyappa to transport anything edible when he was carrying toxic chemicals in his vehicle. Joyappa anticipated a leisurely break with his friend. Plus, he wanted to be a good host and knew that both Joe and he would require some sort of illicit nourishment to fortify themselves after that unsatisfying breakfast.

Joyappa, with Joe in tow, drove his jeep to the little town where he parked on the crowded main road. Joyappa led the way to the little hole-in-the-wall eating place that the owner had grandiosely named 'Five Seasons Café'. Joe was a bit confused, as he was pretty sure that only four seasons existed in his hometown. *Maybe there are more seasons closer to the equator*, he thought. Joyappa motioned for Joe to enter, looked around to ensure that none of Susheela's potential informers had spotted him, and sneaked in to the establishment. Several crude wooden tables with long benches beside them lined the walls. Chomu was seated in a corner of the room, and he greeted Joyappa and Joe enthusiastically.

The first order of business, as far as Joyappa was concerned, was to order some parathas and egg curry—the house speciality. The curry, a yellow viscous substance interspersed with hard boiled eggs, was slopped onto a banana leaf by a sweaty, lungi-clad man with grey chest hair. He was quickly followed by a young fellow attired in loose khaki shorts, who placed oily parathas by the side of the curry. Joe looked around for some silverware and saw none, so he copied Joyappa and Chomu's technique and began to feed himself with his fingers. It was a little awkward at first, but the food was delicious—if a little too spicy. By observing his fellow diners, Joe learned that making eye-contact with the servers followed by a subtle head bobble would get him more food. Many head bobbles later, the three men were finally satisfied. With a raised hand and slight nod, Chomu was able to get a pimply adolescent in the corner to bring them three steel tumblers. The boy expertly filled the tumblers with hot tea from an aluminium kettle. The tea was sweet and milky with a bit of foam on top and, in Joe's opinion, 'hit the spot'.

After their meal, Chomu leaned forward, stroked his prominent lower jaw, and addressed Joe, 'You know, you have a politician with an interesting name. His name is Mitt something or the other—I can't quite remember his surname.'

Joe, who was not exactly interested in politics, was curious, 'Oh, I think I know who you mean. He's a prominent guy, but I can't remember his last name or which party he belongs to. What's so interesting in his name?'

'When I was growing up, I knew a fellow named Mittu. He was a very friendly sort of chap. I lost touch with him after he joined the army. In fact, I have an uncle named Mittu and one of my neighbours is a Mittu—all really nice, friendly fellows who'd give you the shirts off their backs.'

Joyappa, who was rubbing his belly as he idly stared at a lizard on the opposite wall, suddenly tuned in to the conversation. 'I knew the Mittu who joined the army,' he said. 'He was so friendly that I always wondered how he would fight the enemy. There was another Mittu in high school, remember? He was quite the comedian. He kept us amused by imitating the teachers. Chomu, you're absolutely right. If that Mittu fellow ever becomes US president, he will probably make sure that America buys all of our coffee at a premium price.'

Chomu nodded knowingly, much like a political pundit one sees on TV. Joe scratched his head, but try as he might, was unable to follow the warped logic.

Joyappa suddenly glanced at his watch and said, 'We'd better pick up that pesticide and head back or Susheela might get suspicious.'

Chomu looked crestfallen. He was enjoying the company and wanted to have more discussions about America with Joe. Joyappa noticed Chomu's disappointment and said, 'Choms, why don't you come home and spend the day with us?'

'That's okay, Joya,' he replied quickly, since he was quite scared of Susheela. 'Maybe we can go for a trek or something tomorrow and show Joe around?' he added, hopefully.

'Hey, that sounds like fun,' said Joe.

Joyappa nodded in agreement and said, 'We'll call you in the morning, Choms. Maybe we can get Charlie to join us, too. And while you're at it, why don't you organize some refreshments?'

VIII

After breakfast the next morning, Joyappa informed Susheela that he was taking their guest for a short trek to show him some of the local flora and fauna. Susheela was a bit pre-occupied as she prepared materials needed to tutor some of the children in the village, and didn't pay much attention to her husband.

'That's good, dear. Show Joe around, but make sure you bring him back safely,' she said absent-mindedly.

Joyappa gave Joe a satisfied look and they prepared to leave. Given that it was a bright, sunny day both men wore loose shorts, tee shirts and tennis shoes. Joe slipped on his designer sunglasses. Joyappa may have neglected to take hats for the trek, but he didn't forget to put on his aviator sunglasses before getting in to the jeep.

They drove to a poorly maintained estate several kilometres away. The property was adjacent to a game sanctuary and belonged to a wealthy relative of Joyappa's, who lived in Bangalore. About half of the estate had been planted with cardamom and was now overrun with weeds. The rest of the land was uncultivated and consisted of dense vegetation that was indistinguishable from the nearby jungle.

Chomu was already there, periodically looking at his watch as he paced back and forth. Upon seeing them his face lit up, 'Guys, you're seven minutes late. Charlie said he couldn't come. I think he's gone a little soft in the head. He gave me some lame excuse about his fiancé being in town.'

'Hey, Choms! It's too bad Charlie couldn't make it. He'd have liked to meet Joe.'

Chomu removed a large plastic ice cooler from the back of his jeep, 'We'd better get moving before it gets even hotter,' he said.

They entered the property in single file with Joyappa leading the way. Chomu slung the heavy cooler on his back, and Joe brought up the rear. The mixture of native and non-native trees lining the path afforded some shade, and the three men set off in good spirits. After a while, Joyappa wished he'd worn trousers instead of shorts as he encountered overgrown, thorny shrubs that scratched his exposed legs. He also wished that he'd brought along a knife. He picked up a stout stick instead, and cleared the way.

Chomu decided to educate Joe about the various trees they saw. Although he was quite familiar with the local names of the trees, Chomu's knowledge of scientific nomenclature was limited. Typically, ignorance proved no obstacle to his eloquence. So a *Dalbergia* was incorrectly called a *Terminalia*, a huge *Tectona* was erroneously termed an *Albizzia*, a young, fruiting *Artocarpus* had the misfortune of being identified as a *Pterocarpus*, while an imposing *Lagerstroemia* quietly suffered the indignity of being mistaken for an *Erythrina*. It was all Latin to Joe, whose knowledge of biology (from years of weightlifting) was restricted to the effect of protein supplements on muscle size. Nevertheless, he was fascinated by the flora, which was so different from the vegetation of his country.

As they began a gentle climb up the hill, Chomu got winded and mercifully stopped talking. Noticing his discomfort, Joe offered to carry the heavy ice cooler, which Chomu gratefully handed over.

Joe also noticed that the trees were more sparsely distributed and considerably shorter than at the base of the mountain. The single cloud, that had obscured the sun for much of the morning, moved away, allowing the sun to beat down on the parched landscape. Perspiration began to roll off the bodies of the three men.

Since Joe had just spent a long, cold winter in sun-starved northern latitudes, exposure to the tropical sun was beginning to take a toll on him. He also hadn't broken in his new tennis shoes and began to develop several blisters on his feet. When he saw a narrow stream that they had to cross, he said, 'Hey, guys, do you mind if we stop for a bit?'

'Sure, Joe,' said Joyappa without turning around.

He splashed water over his face and head and proceeded to sit in the shade with his back against a rock. Chomu followed suit. He was out of breath and, uncharacteristically, didn't have anything to say. Joe removed his shoes and dipped his sore, blistered feet in the cool stream. It felt wonderful. He also splashed water on himself, before lying in the shade.

Chomu pulled out a packet of cigarettes and offered one to Joyappa. Joyappa had been trying to quit for a long time, so he shook his head. Chomu then turned to ask Joe if he wanted one, when he had a major shock and almost screamed in fear. Joe's face bore a striking resemblance to a ripe tomato.

His normal complexion was very pale, and like most redheads, his skin tended to burn easily. So the sudden exposure to the intense tropical sun had caused the uncovered parts of his body to turn red.

'*My God, Joe*! What happened to you, man?'

'What do you mean?' said Joe, puzzled.

'Your face. It's different. Are you feeling well?'

'Oh, I'm fine, Chomu. I'm guessing that I got a little sunburned. It's nothing to worry about.'

'If you say so,' said Chomu, unconvinced. 'Cigarette?'

'No thanks. I used to smoke in high school—and a bit in college. It's tempting, but I shouldn't.'

Looking concerned, since he hadn't seen anyone turn so red after what he considered a brief exposure to sunlight, Joyappa said, 'Sorry I didn't get you a hat, Joe. Would you like to turn back?'

'Naah. I should be fine.'

Chomu lit up a cigarette and began to puff away contentedly. The smell of burning tobacco was too much to resist and first Joyappa, then Joe, succumbed to temptation. Chomu also distributed cans of cool beer to add to their pleasure.

'We've got about an hour of trekking—mostly uphill, Joe. There's a spot halfway up the hill with a natural rock pool from where there's a great view of the Western Ghats. I thought we could have lunch there, relax and head back when we feel like.'

Joe said, 'Sounds good, Joy.'

Then Joyappa decided to get in a dig. 'Of course, if it is too hard for you, Joe, we can always turn back. After all, American football players aren't exposed to anything—what with all that protection, they probably cry like babies when they're hurt.'

Joe Scurlock became angry. He quickly stubbed out his cigarette, drained the beer and got to his feet. He crushed the empty beer can against his forehead, and with blue eyes flashing, said, 'Go ahead, guys. Let's climb the damn hill.'

Joyappa picked up the cooler and led the way. Both he and Chomu were finding the going tough, but at least they were used to the heat. Joe, on the other hand, was struggling. The heat was bothering him, the blisters on his feet burned agonizingly and his previously injured knee had begun to ache. But he kept going. In fact, after making that joke about field hockey players being wimps, he now had the sacred duty to uphold the honour of the American football player.

Adding to Joe's misery, Chomu had recovered sufficiently to start talking again. This time the topic was birds. While Joe appreciated seeing several unfamiliar birds in the wild, Chomu unnecessarily pointed out a peacock, a crow and a woodpecker. Since his knowledge was restricted to just these common species, Chomu pretended not to notice the Paradise Fly Catchers, green pigeons, castor pigeons, rock doves, bull finches and crow-pheasants that they passed. Joe didn't bother to ask about the birds' names as he just wanted Chomu to shut up.

Joyappa pointed out a Malabar giant squirrel high up in a wild fig tree, and a sleek mongoose that ran across their path. Along the way, they saw the hoof prints of a gaur (bison) and the droppings of a big cat, probably a panther; however, they didn't actually spot any large animals. As they neared their destination, the sun was blazing down and the three men were exhausted. Joe and Joyappa were walking with pronounced limps, while clouds of mosquitoes hovered around all of them, periodically settling on exposed flesh and adding to their discomfort.

Finally, about halfway up the hill, they rounded a corner, forced their way through a few metres of waist-high brush and found themselves at their destination. Joyappa and Chomu reached the spot a few minutes before Joe. Joyappa had not exaggerated. The place *was* beautiful.

The stream that originated near the top of the hill formed a little waterfall about fifty metres away. Thereafter, it ran across a gently sloping piece of land, entered a large, rock-lined pool, and continued its downward journey. The boughs of a few stunted trees overhung parts of the pool, thus providing shade. At the base of these trees grew a wide assortment of ferns, the likes of which Joe had never seen before. From where they stood, the view of the mountains and plains below was spectacular.

Joe was feeling quite proud of himself. Despite his burly frame, the old knee injury and the brutal tropical sun, he had somehow managed to keep up with his hosts and avoid giving them an opportunity to stomp on the reputation of American athletes.

The water was clear and inviting, and it wasn't long before the men had shed their clothes and jumped in. As they looked out at the mountains, it seemed to Joe that nature had designed the most beautiful infinity pool imaginable.

Soon, the men were sitting in the shallow part of the pool, puffing away at cigarettes, chugging beers and letting the clear mountain water cool their bodies. When he began to feel better, Joe noticed tiny fish darting around and pointed them out to Chomu.

'Yes, those little fellows make for a great pickle and a decent curry,' said Chomu. 'They're usually caught in baskets placed at a narrow part of the stream; the water flows through and the fish get trapped.'

'Is that right?' said Joe, who had already experienced Chomu's tendency to exaggerate.

'Yes, Joe,' confirmed Joyappa, 'they're called *koile meen*, and if prepared right, they *are* delicious.'

'Yes, they're really tasty. But cleaning them is tedious—it requires a microscope, you know,' lied Chomu with a straight face.

At this point, Joe was showing further effects of his exposure to the sun. A seafood aficionado might have seen in Joe a strong resemblance to a lobster; however, both Joyappa and Chomu thought he resembled a well cooked tandoori chicken. The thought of chicken made them hungry, so they climbed out of the pool and allowed their bodies to dry in the warm air before eating.

Lunch, extracted from Chomu's box of goodies, was simple. It had been prepared by Chomu's cook and was quite different from any picnic fare Joe had previously consumed. There was lightly spiced ghee-rice speckled with raisins and served with homemade lime pickle. A cooling, lightly seasoned raitha—made from cucumber and onions in a yoghurt base—contrasted with the spicy kick of the pickle. The meal was embellished with smoked, sun-dried meat. Joyappa suspected it was illegally obtained venison; whereas Chomu was evasive about the source. The meat had been cut into thin strips, fried with onions and delicately flavoured with spices.

Hunger, as Joyappa's grandmother had been fond of telling him, is the best sauce. The men were ravenous after their exertions and ate heartily until the food was finished. They also polished off all of the beer, since they decided that carrying back a heavy cooler just didn't make much sense.

Joe couldn't think of a prettier spot or a more delicious meal. Chomu distributed some cigars and the men slipped back in the water and puffed away in silence, as the water gently lapped against their round, exposed bellies—two of which were brown and hairy, and the other, pink, freckled and shiny.

After relaxing for a while, they reluctantly donned their clothes and made their way down the hill. Chomu led the way back, and was uncharacteristically quiet. They found the walk back much less tiring, although Joe had to tread carefully because of his blistered feet.

As they neared the bottom of the hill, the path curved around and was lined with thick *Lantana* shrubs. Chomu turned around and noticed that Joe was about fifty metres behind and treading gingerly. He decided that it was the perfect time to make a crack about the toughness of American football players.

'Hey, Joe,' shouted Chomu, 'About those skirts-,' but he did not finish his thought.

There was a sudden rustling in the undergrowth and the hikers caught a fleeting glimpse of a massive, dark grey mass as it burst onto the path from their right side, ran between Chomu and Joyappa and disappeared into the vegetation on the opposite side.

Joe was at a relatively safe distance, but could still hear the thundering hooves and marvel at the speed and power of the animal as it crashed through the bushes. Chomu returned to earth after a tremendous, gravity-defying vertical leap. Joyappa instinctively dropped the empty cooler in his hands and crossed his hands protectively over his nether regions. Both men looked pale and dazed.

'*Holy Mackarel!* What the heck was that?' said Joe.

'Wild boar,' said Joyappa shakily, as he came out of his defensive posture and bent to pick up the cooler. 'Very dangerous. Lots of hunters have been gored where one wouldn't want to be gored.'

'Man, I can believe it. It was incredibly powerful and fast. And the tusks on the guy—*Geez!*'

They resumed their trek much more cautiously. A few minutes later, after the colour had returned to his face, Chomu stuck out his jaw and said, 'Hey, Joe. That was a relatively small fellow. A few years ago, I was on the estate teaching some new workers how to prune coffee. Suddenly, a boar burst out of some weeds straight at us. Oh, that one was about twice the size of the one we just saw. I was a bit surprised, as you might expect, but I took care of things.'

'What do you mean, "took care of things"?' asked Joe.

'The boar was going right at one of my men, so I clapped to distract him—the boar, I mean. He turned his beady little eyes towards me and charged directly at, um, the family jewels. I just stepped out of the way and stuck a leg out to trip him. He came down with a crash. Before he could get up, I pinned him down and finished him off with my pruning knife. It *was* a bit messy, but I didn't have much of a choice, did I?'

'I suppose not,' said Joe, doubtfully, as he looked at Joyappa.

Joyappa rolled his eyes, and winked. He wondered how Chomu concocted these stories so effortlessly. One look at Chomu's coffee plants would illustrate that his knowledge of pruning left much to be desired. As far as the tale about the giant wild boar—it was so unlikely that he didn't dignify it with a response.

When they reached their vehicles, Joe and Joyappa thanked Chomu for the supplies, since they had genuinely enjoyed the alcohol, tobacco and lunch. Chomu looked a bit sad when they parted, but he turned down Joyappa's invitation to dinner when he heard that Susheela was expected back later that evening.

Susheela was already back when they drove up to the house. 'Oh, oh,' muttered Joyappa, 'I'm going to be in big trouble.'

He asked Joe to enter the house while he parked the jeep in the garage. Then, Joyappa headed for the back of the house, quickly entered the kitchen, sneaked into their bedroom and charged for the safety of the bathroom.

In the meanwhile, Susheela was staring in shock at their guest. Every visible inch of Joe's skin was incredibly red. His eyes looked very blue (and sheepish) against his sunburned face. Also, contrasting with the redness of his thick legs were several greyish-black lumps. Closer observation by Susheela revealed that they were leeches. If *that* wasn't enough, Joe exuded an overpowering odour of sweat, tobacco and beer.

'*Goodness!* What happened to you, Joe?' whispered Susheela, 'What on earth would Patty say if we were to send you back in this deplorable condition?'

Susheela knew that the culprit would have to be taken to task. '*Joy!*' she shouted, '*I want to talk to you RIGHT NOW!*'

When Joyappa heard his wife scream, he turned on the shower and started to sing loudly. As he began to remove a particularly stubborn leech from between his toes, he hoped that Susheela's anger would subside by the time he finished cleaning up. Joyappa showered for a very, very long time. After drying himself, he further extended his stay in the bathroom by coating his body with Susheela's expensive moisturizer and dousing himself with cologne. In anticipation of the impending confrontation, he spent several minutes in front of the bathroom mirror practising a look of extreme innocence.

When Joyappa *finally* emerged after his prolonged stay in the bathroom, he was squeaky clean, with baby-soft, fragrant skin. Predictably, Susheela gave him a severe tongue-lashing about how irresponsible he had been with their guest. Joyappa just hung his head and looked at his toes. He knew she was angry since her face was flushed, a vein throbbed near her left temple and her lips moved rapidly. Fortunately, he had stuffed his ears with cotton wool so he couldn't hear anything she said. When she finished with her tirade, Susheela directed a final, venomous glare at him, tossed her head and stormed out of the room. Joyappa discreetly removed his ear plugs and began to read the sports section of the newspaper.

IX

The next day, Susheela prepared an extract from Aloe vera leaves that, to Joe's surprise, was very soothing. However, his skin stayed red for a few days, after which it began to peel. Susheela was very concerned that Joe's injuries were permanent, and tried to get him treated professionally. Predictably, none of the local doctors had any experience treating severe sunburn. A friend suggested that Susheela contact a retired physician who lived in a village nearby. So she took Joe to see the old man who had treated Caucasians for similar ailments around the time of Independence.

The old doctor looked at Joe's red, peeling skin and said, 'My, my! It has been a very long time since I've seen a case of sunburn that bad. Takes me back to the old days when the Britishers who came here during the winter got burned by the tropical sun. Oh, I treated a lot of such cases. I also treated a number of them for stomach problems. Do you have stomach problems, too, Mr Scurlock?'

'Um, no.'

'Fine, fine. Then, I'll mix up something that I used to in the old days,' said the doctor, before tottering off to another room where Susheela and Joe could hear the sounds of bottles being opened and liquids being mixed. When he returned, the doctor handed over an amber bottle filled with a thick fluid to Joe, along with several tablets wrapped in a small piece of newspaper.

'Apply this lotion to your skin twice a day,' said the doctor. 'Also take one tablet after breakfast and the other just before you go to bed, and you should be fine in a few days.'

'Sure thing, Doc. Thanks for your help.'

'Don't mention it, Mr Spurlick. I once treated someone from Ireland who looked like you. Didn't you say you were from Ireland?'

'Nope. Doc, I said I was from–,' Joe stopped in mid-sentence because the doctor sat down abruptly, rested his head on the desk and began to snore gently.

Susheela left some money on the table before she led Joe out. As they drove back home, she hoped the old man had not given Joe medicines for 'Delhi Belly' by mistake, which would lead to a completely different set of problems.

Meanwhile, Joyappa was on the estate, pretending to supervise work. Susheela was so preoccupied with the state of their guest that she hadn't really nagged Joyappa as much as he expected. While his workers pruned coffee, Joyappa wandered away to a secluded part of the property to smoke. He was in enough trouble and didn't want any disgruntled employees going behind his back and telling Susheela about his tobacco addiction.

As Joyappa sat in the shade of a leafy neem tree and lit up, he noticed that a portion of the *Jatropha* hedge along the boundary of the property had been flattened, leaving a large gap. When he went closer to investigate, he saw a couple of enormous footprints that could only mean one thing— *elephants!*

Joyappa stepped on his cigarette and tried to see if there had been any damage to his coffee plants. After breaking through the hedge, the elephants had evidently walked along a mud road, but the hard, sun-baked surface prevented him from tracking them. Following some aimless wandering (and several cigarettes), he came across a few damaged coffee bushes and several large seeds strewn about the base of a large jackfruit tree. He concluded that the elephants had shaken the tree to dislodge the ripe fruits. In the process, a few branches of the coffee bushes in the vicinity had been broken, but the damage was not as severe as it could have been.

Joyappa realized that they had been fortunate, as elephants very rarely entered their property. However, over the past couple of years, wild bamboo in the nearby forests had flowered after several decades of vegetative growth, and subsequently died. The bamboo seeds that had fallen to the forest floor would take years to grow into plants large enough to provide sufficient biomass to keep the elephants sated. The absence of this major food source forced the animals to stray into cultivated lands looking for fruits, rice and other vegetation to satisfy their enormous appetites.

Given that most people in the area were well aware of the lifespan of wild bamboo, Joyappa and other planters often wondered why no measures had been taken to plant bamboo and other sources of food in a staggered manner to ensure that wild herbivores had a steady source of nutrition in the forests. Further, as a means to generate revenue, vast areas of the jungle had been cleared and replanted with teak. Teak trees were a source of fine timber, but unfortunately, discouraged growth of bamboo and other native species in their vicinity.

Reports had been filtering in from various parts of the district of elephants destroying acres and acres of crops in their quest for food. Several unfortunate people had been trampled, gored or flung through the air by elephants. Many elephants, in turn, had been killed upon coming in contact with low hanging power lines, or shot by farmers protecting their crops and lives. Yet, hunger and loss of habitat continued to drive the elephants towards cultivated areas, and therefore human habitation, resulting in many unfortunate incidents.

It was with a worried look that Joyappa returned home for lunch. The curtains were drawn leaving the room in partial darkness. Joe was lying on the couch watching a basketball game on TV.

'Hey, Joy. How's it going?'

Joyappa took a moment to respond since he was taken unawares by Joe's appearance. Joe's skin was coated with some sort of whitish paste through which Joyappa could see his peeling skin. The view was a bit shocking, but he managed to reply, 'Hello Joe. How are you feeling?'

Joe dropped his voice and said, 'Not too bad, Joy. You know, I appreciate Sue's concern and everything. But man, I'd rather be hanging out with you and Chomu. I'm getting kinda tired of being cooped up like this. Sue won't even let me step outside for a few minutes.'

Joyappa nodded sympathetically. He knew quite well how it felt to have one's personal freedom curtailed. Unfortunately, he wasn't sure how he could solve Joe's problem, since he himself was in the proverbial 'doghouse'.

Over lunch, Joyappa mentioned that one or more elephants had entered the estate and fed on jackfruit. Susheela was concerned about both human safety and damage to the estate.

Joe, on the other hand, not quite realizing the gravity of the situation, looked excited. His eyes lit up behind the white paste that coated his face, and he said, 'I haven't seen an elephant yet in the wild. Mind if I go with you, Joy, so we can check it out?'

'Joy,' said Susheela, in a voice that brooked no argument, 'you will *NOT* be taking Joe on any more foolhardy adventures. We will send him back to Patty in one piece. You have done quite enough damage already. Thank heavens your pal Chomu wasn't there when you took Joe on that foolish trek.'

Joyappa didn't reply, he just looked down at his plate and started to put some bland, boiled vegetables in his mouth. He was hoping that Joe would have enough sense not to tell Susheela that Chomu had, in fact, been on the trek and was instrumental in supplying forbidden materials for their excursion. Joyappa need not have worried. Joe, too, was looking down at his plate wondering how he could get out of his present situation as a virtual prisoner and have some fun with the guys.

Joe's prayers were answered shortly after lunch. The phone

rang and Susheela answered. The men could hear her say, 'I'm sorry to hear that, Mummy. We have a guest at the moment. He's my friend Patty's husband and is visiting from the States. If he doesn't mind, I can drive up to be with you for a couple of days. I think Joy will be able to take care of things for that long.'

Susheela hung up a few minutes later. She turned to Joe, and looking very apologetic, said, 'My mother just called to say that she's sprained an ankle. She's been asked to keep her leg elevated and wondered if I could spend a couple of days helping out. I know it isn't right of me to leave you by yourselves, but I hope you don't mind if I head off to my parents' place?'

Joe had to exercise iron self-control to keep from jumping up and down with relief. He managed to look suitably disappointed when he said, 'Oh Sue, we'll miss you for sure, but you'd better get to your folks' place right away. I'll be fine. The doctor's medicine seems to be working great. *Please* go ahead.'

Joyappa also decided to help Susheela with her decision, 'Yes, Susheela, Joe's right. You *must* get going to help your mother. Joe will be just fine—I'll keep an eye on him.'

'Thanks, fellows,' said Susheela gratefully. 'I'm really sorry to leave like this. Joe, try to make yourself comfortable and I'll rush back as soon as I can.'

X

After Susheela drove off, Joe again asked Joyappa if he would take him to spot wild elephants. Joyappa said that it was highly unlikely that the elephants would be on the estate during the day. He explained that in all probability, the elephants entered the property late at night, and tried to find something to eat before returning to the jungle or an abandoned plantation before daylight.

'Well, in that case, maybe we can look for them at night,' said Joe enthusiastically.

'Too dangerous, Joe. While *we* don't scare them away, there are people who burst crackers or even shoot at them. So they could well be jumpy and unpredictable. Despite their size, they move around very silently and we could get within touching distance of an elephant without knowing it. Believe me! You do not want to be chased by an angry elephant.'

'Aww, c'mon man, Joy. It'll be a lot of fun.'

Joyappa was adamant. He wasn't going to risk Susheela's wrath if anything further happened to Joe. Actually being chased by an angry elephant might be more pleasant.

A very disappointed Joe said, 'At least we could meet up with Chomu this evening.'

'Yes, we could do that,' said Joyappa. He felt a little guilty that he hadn't returned a couple of Chomu's calls because he had been preoccupied with his attempts to avoid being nagged by Susheela. So he dialled Chomu and said, 'Hey, Choms, you want to come over for a drink today?'

Chomu hemmed and hawed and made up excuses about an appointment with a fertilizer dealer. In reality, he didn't want to meet Susheela. But, he was also lonely and anxious for some company, so he said, 'Maybe you can bring Joe over to my place.'

'I don't know if we can leave since Susheela is going to be away for a couple of days, and Joe probably needs to rest.'

Chomu's response was swift and unambiguous, 'I'll be there in a jiffy, Joya.'

'What about your appointment?'

'What appointment?'

'The one you just mentioned with the fertilizer dealer.'

'Oh, that,' said Chomu, remembering his excuse, 'I'll reschedule. I'm on my way right now, Joya, so don't leave your place.'

Chomu arrived in a remarkably short time. He had been feeling lonely after the trek and was very happy to have some company again. When he slapped Joe on the back in a friendly way, Joe actually jumped, as his sunburn had not healed completely. Upon entering the house, Chomu checked the dining room, kitchen and Joyappa's bedroom to confirm that Susheela was not, in fact, in the house. Thereafter, he went back to his car and brought out his cooler. Bottles of beer were quickly opened and the three men sat around a table upon which they rested their feet, shoes and all.

'So, what's that white stuff on your face, Joe?' asked Chomu.

'Something a doctor prescribed for sunburn. Sue took me to this old doctor's house and the guy gave me some salve to put on my skin.'

'Huh,' said Chomu, 'if only you had told me you required treatment, I would have mixed up a traditional remedy for you.'

Joyappa was curious. He had never heard of any such remedy. In fact, he couldn't recall hearing of anyone being sunburned in the district.

'Oh, yeah?' said Joe, who was obviously very interested, as his light skin tended to burn easily even in temperate conditions.

Chomu took a long swig of beer. He stuck out his jaw aggressively, parked his sunglasses on his head and said, 'Yes. I learned the secret from an old tribal woman many years ago.

You'd first have to find a pregnant cow. Mind you, it would have to be a local breed—Holsteins and Jerseys won't do. Collect the urine first thing in the morning in an earthen pot. Pour it back and forth between two metal cups until it has a nice head on it. Mix in some turmeric powder and let the stuff sit in the shade for exactly twelve and a half minutes.'

Joyappa was beginning to look skeptical. Chomu paused to take another swallow of beer.

Joe, who was paying close attention, asked, 'Is that it?'

Chomu wiped his moustache for effect and looked around at his audience. 'Ha! Is that it? Is *that* it? Well, it certainly isn't,' he said. 'Next, you'd have to collect the saliva from a dog—not a bitch or a castrated dog, but from a vigorous male. Remember, a local breed is essential. The saliva of a Rajapalayam would do, but not a labradog or a hairdale or any of those fancy breeds.'

Now that Chomu was on a roll, in addition to mispronouncing the names of canine breeds, he also started to confuse them with mango varieties. He continued with great assurance, 'A Banganapalli or a Dussheri would also be a good source of saliva, but that of a Rajapalayam would be best. Three teaspoons of saliva, a dash of cashew *feni* and it's ready to go.'

Joyappa had tuned out and had already started on his second bottle of beer. Joe looked at Chomu, wide-eyed. He wondered how he would be able to lay his hands on all these exotic ingredients if the need arose. His knowledge of sub-continental geography was poor, so he didn't really question how a traditional remedy from a tribal who lived deep in the south called for *feni*—a drink brewed on the west coast.

'That sounds, ghastly, man. What next?' asked Joe.

'Well, it's up to the patient. You could add salt to taste and drink it. Or, you could smear it all over your body. Either way it is very, very effective.'

Joyappa decided to change subjects since he knew if Chomu proceeded unchecked, he could go on for hours and the stories would become progressively more absurd. 'We've had elephants in the estate,' he said to Chomu, 'they caused some damage while raiding a jackfruit tree near the boundary.'

'Hey, Chomu, I was telling Joy that I would really like to see jumbos in their natural habitat,' said Joe.

Joyappa mentally kicked himself and wished he'd brought up some other topic so that Joe wasn't reminded about his desire to see wild elephants.

'No problem, Joe. We can arrange to have you see all the elephants you want,' said Chomu.

Joyappa was horrified. He remembered Susheela's warning about keeping Joe safe. He tried to cut Chomu off, but to no avail.

'I'll tell you what we can do to see some elephants up close. First we'll build a small tree house or machan on the very same jackfruit tree that the elephants visited. If there are more ripe fruits on it, the elephants are bound to be back. So we get to see them from close quarters and also have a guy's night out.'

'But—,' said Joyappa trying to stop Chomu from talking, but before he could finish, Joe quickly said, 'Chomu, that's an absolutely fantastic idea.'

Chomu and Joe then began to talk loudly and excitedly, giving Joyappa no chance to dissuade them. Joyappa eventually gave up and secretly became quite enthusiastic about the idea.

'Fellows,' said Joyappa, 'if we are doing this, you have to swear not to utter a word about it to Susheela.'

'I'm pretty darn sure that I'm not tellin' Sue about it. She's bound to tell my wife everything and I don't want to be nagged for six months after I get home.'

'Joya, I assure you that I would rather neuter myself with a blunt knife than tell Susheela about our plan,' said Chomu—and Joyappa believed him.

The rest of the afternoon was spent in the planning and construction of the machan. Joe was asked to stay at home since Joyappa didn't want him to be scorched any further by the afternoon sun. Joyappa assigned the job to two of his trusted workers, Mani and Naga. Over the years, Joyappa had kept them happy by slipping them a little extra money during weekly payments. These men didn't squeal to Susheela about his occasional indulgence in terms of drinking toddy or smoking on the estate, so he was confident that news of his illicit activities would not spread.

Being skilled at pruning trees, Mani and Naga quickly shimmied up the jackfruit tree that the elephants had visited. A fork high up in the tree served as the base of the structure. Dry bamboo poles and wooden planks of red cedar were lashed together with rope to form the flooring. An old, green tarpaulin was used to provide shelter overhead. The final product was a simple structure, open on all four sides, that was wide enough for three people. The tarpaulin would provide some shelter from dew or rain. Once Joyappa and Chomu had approved the machan, the workers descended. Joyappa asked them to bring a traditional bamboo ladder, consisting of a long pole with small rungs along the sides, and place it against the tree.

Susheela had prepared chappatis and a vegetable fry for dinner, so all Joyappa had to do was heat it up. It wasn't particularly appealing to any of the men, so Joyappa whipped up a massive, twelve egg omelet to supplement the meal. The men ate quickly as they were excited about their impending adventure and wanted to get to the machan before dark. Joyappa tried to think of the essentials they would need for the night and filled a bag with a couple of torches, an electric lantern, a battery powered lamp that was meant to be worn on one's head, cigarettes, a pack of beedis, matches, playing cards, some chocolate biscuits and several bottles of rum. He also took his double-barreled shotgun—just in case.

Upon leaving the house, Joyappa summoned Mani and had him accompany them to the jackfruit tree. Mani held the base of the bamboo ladder to provide support. Chomu was first to climb up. He huffed and puffed but made it to the top safely with the bag of supplies. Joyappa was next. He slung the strap of his shotgun over his shoulder and started off confidently. When he was halfway up the ladder, the injured knee locked up, and his foot slipped off a rung. He hung on tightly and managed to place his foot back on the ladder. He rested for a minute until his knee loosened up before he climbed the rest of the way. The evening's first setback occurred when Joe began to climb the ladder. When he was about eight feet off the ground and making good progress, his enormous weight caused one of the rungs to break. Joe's leg slipped and as he hung on to the bamboo pole, it creaked, then bowed a little, and finally shattered. Joe hit the ground with a massive thud.

Joyappa's heart was in his mouth. Besides concern for his guest, he was worried about getting Susheela upset. What would

Susheela say if Joe was badly injured? What kind of elaborate excuse would he have to fabricate?

Fortunately, Joe picked himself up, dusted himself off and said, 'Dang! That was one flimsy ladder. How the heck am I to get up there, now, guys?'

Mani thought for a moment, then picked up a knife and began to climb the tree. He cut shallow notches along the surface of the tree all the way to the machan, before rapidly descending to the ground. Mani indicated to Joe that he should try to climb the tree using the notches as footholds. Joe nodded approvingly at the idea, although Joyappa and Chomu were very concerned. Joe grabbed the tree and placed his feet in the footholds. To everyone's surprise, he climbed quite nimbly.

Upon reaching the top, despite being winded, he grinned happily, exchanged high fives with Joyappa and Chomu, and said, 'All those years of practice on a 'climbing wall' in the college gym paid off, I guess.'

Joyappa asked Mani to leave before it got dark and the men on the machan settled down to wait. In the late evening light, several colourful crotons along the boundary appeared to glow in spectacular fashion. Joe and Joyappa quietly enjoyed the tranquil atmosphere in silence. As Chomu began to talk, Joyappa, who didn't want to hear yet another incredible story, quickly shushed him saying that too much noise would scare away the elephants.

When it became dark, Joyappa switched on the electric lantern, pulled out a couple of decks of cards and asked Joe if he would like to play. Joe said he would, but they couldn't decide on a game that all three of them knew to play. Clearly, anything requiring memory and skill was unlikely to be their first choice, so Chomu decided to teach Joe 'bluff'—a simple game that relied on one's ability to lie to one's competitors with a straight face. Predictably, Chomu won every game they played. There's little doubt he would have won anyway, but Chomu made doubly sure of victory by hiding some cards in his underwear.

When they tired of the card game, Joyappa realized that he was feeling a bit hungry. So he stretched out and picked a couple of ripe jackfruits that were hanging from a nearby branch. He tapped each of them with a fingernail, listened closely and chose the smaller of the two fruits. After Chomu cut open the spiky, green surface with a pocket knife, the men stuck their hands in and began to eat the sticky, yellow flesh. Initially, Joe found the strong, sweet odour overpowering, but it didn't bother him for long and he tucked in with gusto. The large seeds were just thrown off the machan and landed at the base of the tree. When they couldn't eat any more, the remaining fruit was also disposed off in the same way.

By now, hungry mosquitoes had begun to feast on them. Joyappa wished he'd brought along some insect repellent, but in its absence decided to improvise. He lit and distributed the beedis that he had packed earlier. When Joe first inhaled, he couldn't stop coughing as the acrid smoke from the crude tobacco hit his lungs. Eventually, he seemed to get used to it and the three men puffed away happily. Joyappa was pleased that the pungent smoke kept the mosquitoes at bay.

When they finished the beedis, the men felt thirsty. Unfortunately, they had forgotten to bring water. Since it would not have been safe to climb down the tree and collect water in the dark, Joyappa pulled out a few 'quarter' bottles of rum, which he duly distributed. In companionable silence, the adventurers swigged large amounts of neat liquor.

Joyappa found that the night had become cool, and regretted that he hadn't brought any blankets. Joe, however, having just been through a frigid North American winter, felt it was a bit warm and removed his shirt. In anticipation of his first elephant sighting, he placed his smartphone with its fancy camera by his side, and lay down on the wooden planks. Soon Joyappa and Chomu also stretched out on the floor of the machan. The mosquitoes had returned in force and began to feed on them with a vengeance. But the alcohol had kicked in and none of the men felt any discomfort from either the mosquito attack or the hard wooden surface upon which they rested.

Chomu initially suggested that they stay up all night and the others agreed. However, full bellies and the rum caused them to feel sleepy. As he dozed off, Joyappa thought to himself that a little nap wouldn't hurt. After all, if the elephants were to visit, he was sure he would hear them. Soon, the three men were sound asleep.

A couple of hours later, Joe Scurlock began to dream that he was sailing on Lake Erie, that vast expanse of water stretching between Canada and the United States. He dreamt that the strong winds from the north were whipping up the water as he struggled to keep the little sailboat from capsizing. Joyappa dreamt that he was sitting in a comfortable rocking chair watching professional wrestling on TV. Not to be left out, Chomu was enjoying a dream that elicited a happy smile—but the poor fellow's dream was the most implausible of them all. Chomu dreamt that his wife had returned from the big city and lay (willingly) in his arms.

Several hours later, Joyappa woke upon upon hearing a familiar voice say, 'Sir, sir–'

Joyappa opened his eyes, not quite sure where he was. He lifted his head and groaned. His tongue felt furry and his mouth tasted like one of Susheela's awful curried bitter gourd dishes. As he wiped the sleep from his eyes and remembered that he was on a tree, he wondered why it wasn't dark any more. When he looked down, he could see Mani, gazing anxiously up at him.

'What do you want, Mani?' he asked, grumpily.

'Sir, are you okay?'

'Why do you ask?'

'A herd of elephants must have passed by. They seem to have shaken the tree vigorously since they've eaten a lot of jackfruits down here. Even though the ground is hard, I can see several footprints. They've also broken off the branches of a few orange trees.'

'Mani, don't talk rubbish,' came the stern reply from above. 'Have you been drinking, man?'

'No, sir,' said Mani in a small voice.

'We've been right here all night. Don't you think we would have seen or heard the elephants if they were at the bottom of the tree, shaking it 'til the ripe fruit fell?'

'Sir, I would have expected you to see them.'

'Well, run along and get ready for work. How many times have I told you not to drink on working days, Mani?'

'But–,' Mani began to protest his innocence, then thought better of it and left shaking his head.

Joyappa looked at Joe to see if he was okay. Joe snored

softly as he lay on his stomach. His nose was squashed against the floor of the machan, and his upper lip quivered gently each time he exhaled. Joyappa was shocked to see that Joe's bare back was covered with little red mosquito bites. He tapped Joe on the shoulder and the sleeping man woke with a start.

Both Joyappa and Joe looked at Chomu and saw that he was hugging the large jackfruit that had been picked the previous night. Even Chomu's mother would have had to admit that it didn't make for a pretty sight. Joyappa averted his eyes before shaking his friend awake. Chomu looked sheepish when he realized that he was embracing a fruit, and quickly pushed it away hoping that no one had observed his companion.

Joyappa regretted having sent Mani off without asking him to prop another ladder against the tree. So it was with some difficulty that the three badly hungover men descended. Fortunately, they reached the ground without incurring any injuries.

'Holy Smokes!' said Joe looking at the base of the tree.

More than a dozen half-eaten jackfruits, that had not been there the previous evening, were scattered around. The fruits must have fallen after the elephants shook the tree. Remarkably, the three drunk men on the machan hadn't fallen down with the jackfruit.

'Too bad we missed them,' said Joyappa, feeling slightly remorseful that he'd been so brusque with Mani. 'If we'd been awake, you might have got some great pictures, Joe.'

Chomu said, 'I was awake all night. I meant to tell you that I observed the animals closely. There were three adults and two calves, but you both looked so peaceful that I didn't want to bother you. Also, they looked pretty hungry, so I thought you'd disturb them if you started taking pictures—*that's* why I decided not to wake you up.'

As they walked slowly back to the house, Joe and Joyappa, who had both observed the sleeping Chomu cuddling a fruit, exchanged looks. They rolled their eyes at each other, but had to clutch at their temples as pain shot through their heads. A couple of minutes later, all three of the wannabe wildlife observers grabbed their cramping stomachs as they began to feel the effects of the jackfruit feast.

XI

Much of the day was spent recovering from the night's excesses. Susheela called Joyappa around noon and said that she would have to stay with her mother for a few more days. She was profusely apologetic that she was neglecting their guest from overseas, but Joyappa allayed her fears and said, 'Oh, there's *absolutely* no problem, Susheela. Everything is under control. Joe is applying medicine to his sunburn as per the doctor's advice.'

'I feel so bad to burden you with the full task of entertaining Joe, and the responsibility of making sure that he gets better before he leaves.'

'Don't worry about it, Susheela. And please don't forget to tell your mother that I hope she's back on her feet soon.'

'I'll be sure to tell her that, Joy,' lied Susheela. As a matter of fact, Susheela made every effort to avoid mentioning Joyappa's name in her mother's presence, since she was concerned that it would cause the injured lady's blood pressure to rise.

'How's Joe looking?'

'Much, much better,' said Joyappa, and he, in turn, wasn't being truthful, since Joe looked awful. His peeling skin was now festooned with numerous, tiny red bumps resulting from the mosquito attack. Since Susheela sounded a little guilty about abandoning her duties as hostess, Joyappa decided to try his luck and said, 'Hey, Susheela. Don't you think it would be a good idea to take Joe on a little trip to see a bit more of the country?'

'Well–,' said Susheela, as she thought about the pros and cons of the situation, 'I suppose you *could*, if you make sure you don't do anything silly.' Then her voice hardened, as she continued, 'But remember, Joy, if any harm comes to Joe from your shenanigans, I will hold YOU personally responsible.'

Joyappa was a bit puzzled, since he wasn't sure what his wife meant by 'shenanigans'. In fact, he thought of the various possessions he kept hidden from Susheela, including cigarettes, alcohol and girly magazines, but couldn't recall owning a single shenanigan.

After a brief pause, he said, with a clear conscience, 'Okay, Susheela, don't you worry that pretty head of yours, dear,' and immediately disconnected the phone before permission for the road trip was retracted.

Joyappa asked Joe if he was interested in travelling before Susheela got back, and he responded in the affirmative. Chomu, of course, was enthusiastic about the trip. After discussing several possible options, Joyappa decided that a visit to a resort by a wildlife sanctuary would be just about right in terms of proximity and comfort. Since it was too late in the day to leave, they decided to spend the night at Joyappa's place and set off the following morning. Chomu, who was so reluctant to visit when Susheela was home, now made no move to leave. In fact, he made himself comfortable and quite happily borrowed clothes from Joyappa for the night. Chomu was also the first to pack a bag with requirements for the trip, including clean underwear, a razor and aftershave (all borrowed from his host). Fortunately, Joyappa was able to locate a new toothbrush before Chomu asked to share one.

The evening was a quiet one, as the men recovered from the excesses of the previous night. They watched an old movie about World War II, and slept like logs in spite of having witnessed gory scenes of tank warfare in North Africa, cities going up in flames, and dogfights between the Luftwaffe and the R.A.F. over the English Channel.

When Joyappa woke his guests early the following morning, the weather had changed dramatically. Temperatures had dropped and dark, moisture-laden clouds moved in purposefully from the south-west. Joe was pleasantly surprised, as all he had experienced on his visit was harsh sunshine and uncomfortably hot weather. *Maybe my skin will heal under these overcast conditions*, he thought.

Chomu volunteered to drive his car. Joyappa sat by Chomu, thinking that Joe would be less nervous if he sat at the back. They passed through a densely forested area with bad roads. There was a gradual, but noticeable drop in elevation as they drove out of the district. Chomu drove fast and made little effort to avoid bumps or potholes. He also shook his fist and shouted at anything or anyone in his way.

There was significantly less cloud cover over the plains, and as the sun rose high in the sky, it became uncomfortably hot. Joe felt nervous and a little queasy with the sudden stops and starts, Chomu's swearing and the residual effects of the night on the machan. Several kilometres later, Chomu rolled up the windows and turned on the air conditioning. The effect on Joe was almost immediate. At first, he was grateful for the cool air blowing at him. A minute or so later, he became aware of a most repellent stench that permeated the vehicle. Chomu sniffed the air and wrinkled his nose before looking at Joyappa to see if he was aware of the nasty odour, but Joyappa had dozed off.

Chomu addressed Joe, 'I noticed a rat was getting into the car every night. So, I left some poison on the engine a few days ago. Looks like the poison worked, huh?'

'Is that what that godawful stench is from?' said Joe feeling even more uncomfortable.

'Yeah, definitely. The rat probably got under the bonnet, ate the poison and somehow entered the air conditioning vent, where it died. From the smell of things, and considering the weather, I'd say it's been dead a couple of days.'

'Hmm,' said Joe, thoroughly disgusted.

Chomu looked over his shoulder and was surprised to see that Joe's brow was furrowed and his complexion had assumed an odd shade of green. But Chomu was intent on finishing his story and didn't pay too much attention before continuing, 'You know, Joe. This is nothing. There was one time, when a rat ate some poison and croaked in the glove box. I hadn't driven the car for a while, when I opened the glove box, the stench was so bad that I couldn't get it out of my nostrils or the car for weeks.'

'Unnh,' was all Joe could say.

'Yup,' continued Chomu, nonchalantly. 'It was ghastly; there were thousands of little white maggots feasting happily on that bloated body.'

Joe couldn't take any more. With one hand over his mouth,

he tapped Chomu on the shoulder and desperately pointed to the side of the road. A puzzled Chomu quickly brought the car to a halt. Joe opened the door and literally dived out of the car before vomiting violently all over a recently planted tobacco field.

Joyappa awoke with a start and after seeing Joe throwing up became concerned that his guest had fallen ill. When Chomu explained what had happened, Joyappa glared at him and growled, 'Switch the bloody AC off, you duffer.'

'Okay, okay,' said Chomu, quickly complying with his order. 'Don't get your chaddis in a twist.'

Joe looked a bit sheepish when he got into the car. 'Sorry guys. That sort of thing doesn't usually happen to me.'

Chomu rolled down the windows and turned the air conditioner off. 'That's fine, Joe. It could happen to anyone. You are probably suffering from artocarpitis.'

'*What* itis?' asked Joe and Joyappa simultaneously.

'Some people are immune to the disease. For example, Joya and I were unaffected, but a casual observer might conclude that you have morning sickness after seeing you provide nourishment to those tobacco plants.'

Joyappa appeared to be scared, while Joe looked very worried, 'Oh God! Is there a cure, guys? I have never heard of the disease. Were you immunized as children?'

'Let me explain,' said Chomu, the resident expert on everything, as he drove through the middle of a huge pothole causing everyone's head to hit the roof. 'You see, *Artocarpus* is the Latin name for jackfruit. It is the world's biggest fruit. There are several varieties of jackfruit, and interestingly, flavour and texture of the fruit can vary considerably. Some fruits are bland so people often dip them in honey to add flavor, while others are so sweet that they can be eaten without any additives.'

Chomu paused to drive around a particularly somnolent buffalo in the middle of the road. Thus far, a horticulturist would have been hard pressed to find fault with the botanical aspects of his explanation.

Presently, Chomu continued, 'Joya and I have been eating jackfruit from a very young age. We've eaten a dish made by frying the immature fruit, gorged on ripe fruit, roasted and eaten the seeds, and consumed a sweet, steamed dish made from the flesh of ripe fruits. Hence, I conclude that we are immune to any adverse effects brought about by the consumption of *Artocapus* fruits.'

'Really?' said Joe, wide-eyed.

'Yup. I therefore believe that you have a bad attack of artocarpitis,' said Chomu with such authority that even an experienced doctor would have had to refer to his books from medical school for details of the exotic tropical ailment. Needless to say, the search would have been fruitless as the disease was a product of Chomu's imagination and improvisational ability.

Chomu braked violently to avoid a sprinting mongoose before unnecessarily needling Joe, 'Hey Joe, I thought American football players were tough guys—but I'm surprised you can't walk up a hill without turning red and having your skin peel. And the attack of artocarpitis—what can I say? It was sad to see a big guy puking his guts out like that after smelling a putrefying rat. Hey, Joy, we'd better make sure Joe learns to wear a sari before he leaves Indian shores.'

'That's enough, Chomu,' said Joyappa, who was worried that his guest would get offended.

Joe, who was good natured when he wasn't on a football field, just smiled at Chomu's dig.

'Incidentally, did you know,' said Chomu with the air of a professor in the middle of a lecture, 'that breadfruit is also named *Artocarpus*?'

Neither of Chomu's passengers knew nor cared, but they certainly felt like organizing a mutiny and offloading the man at the helm. The rest of the journey passed uneventfully and Joe enjoyed the scenery.

The resort was by the side of a major river and just a stone's throw away from a dry, deciduous scrub jungle that had been designated a sanctuary. It had been in operation for just a couple of years, but was getting rave reviews from people who visited from all over the world.

Joyappa had reserved a well appointed cottage for his fellow travellers to share. They were pleased to find a large TV in the common area. Joyappa was glad to see that each bedroom had an attached bathroom, so Chomu wouldn't be borrowing his toothbrush or soap.

From the front verandah, the river glistened in the sun as it made its long journey to the sea. In the background, a range of mountains rose abruptly from the plains, their tops wreathed in clouds. The view was pleasant, as was the cool breeze blowing across the verandah. In addition, the food was good and liquor abundant, so Joyappa was lauded for choosing the accommodations. The men played a lot of cards, with 'bluff' being the game of choice, and Chomu racking up the most victories by means both fair and foul.

In the late afternoon, the resort organized a boat ride through the sanctuary. Joe saw his first crocodile as it sunned itself on a rock in the middle of the river. They saw some spotted deer and a pair of the much larger sambar, which reminded Joe of elk in North America. Water birds were abundant and made for a pretty picture as they sat on tree stumps and tree tops. The guide gamely tried to identify every bird he saw, but none of his passengers seemed particularly interested in the names. An hour into the journey, biscuits were served with hot coffee. Joyappa laced the coffee with brandy from a hip flask leaving everyone, including the guide, in a pleasant mood by the time they reached the shore at the resort.

After dinner, Joe played a DVD of a couple of American football games and explained the rules of the sport to Joyappa and Chomu. Both men were interested in the complex strategy employed on both offense and defense as the coaches tried to outwit each other. They were also impressed with the strength and athleticism of the players. Nevertheless, Chomu couldn't keep from getting in a few comments about how much tougher field hockey players were, in comparison to football players. Joe just smiled good naturedly at the ribbing.

Early the next morning, a knock on the door roused Joyappa, who in turn woke his friends for biscuits and hot tea. Half an hour later, a naturalist introduced himself and said that he would serve as their guide that morning. He was attired in camouflage clothing and sported a large pair of binoculars suspended from his pencil-thin neck. The guide seemed to have a cold, since he incessantly wiped his nose on his sleeve as he led the three sleepy men to an open jeep. The ride on the mud roads was bumpy, but the cool morning air felt pleasant and the men began to scan their surroundings for wildlife.

As the undergrowth in the forest had dried up and many

of the trees had shed their leaves, sighting wildlife was much easier than during the monsoon. Spotted deer were abundant and observed the jeep and its occupants without much alarm. A black faced langur bounded across the road before gracefully climbing a tree and watching the jeep. The guide pointed out a sloth bear, which Joe managed to capture on his camera, before it melted into the forest. Joe also photographed a flying squirrel and a circling bird of prey, before they drove towards the shores of the river.

The guide chose a place to park the jeep where it was partly concealed behind some foliage. Due to insufficient rain, the natural ponds and lakes in the forest were dry. So the river was the only source of water for the animals and birds of the jungle. The high-water mark from the previous monsoon showed just how much the waters had receded during the dry season. The guide whispered that because the river was relatively wide and easily accessible to the wildlife, this particular area was an excellent place to spot animals.

The men settled down to wait. Joyappa felt the urge to smoke, but when he pulled out some cigarettes from his pocket the guide's look of disapproval prompted him to put them away. After five minutes, during which the only sign of life were a few water birds on the river, Chomu began to fidget. A further ten minutes elapsed, at which time Joyappa and Joe exchanged disappointed looks, while Chomu gnawed at his fingernails. The naturalist kept scanning the area with his binoculars. Just when Chomu was thinking about shoving the naturalist out and driving off so they could have some breakfast, things began to happen.

There was the sound of twigs breaking and a bull elephant

made his way to the water just a few feet from the jeep. The tusker waded into the river, drank deeply and sprinkled himself with water. He was a magnificent specimen in the prime of life, and sported thick tusks that were several feet long. Joe was fascinated and almost forgot to photograph the animal. The elephant ate some grass that he pulled from the bank before ambling back to the jungle.

'Wow! That was great,' said Joe and everyone nodded in agreement. 'Makes you wonder what would have happened if those elephants had knocked us off that tree house back at your place.' Again, Joyappa and Chomu nodded somberly.

Against the guide's advice, Joe got out of the jeep. He placed his feet in the enormous footmarks left by the elephant. Seeing that his own feet appeared to be positively petite in comparison, he shook his head in awe and said, 'Man, *that* was one massive dude,' before getting back in the jeep.

Within the next hour, a small herd of gaur, four sambar, and a barking deer, all made their way to the river for a drink. Again, Joe captured some fine images on his camera. Minutes later, a sambar's distress call rang out, and the sound of frenzied activity in a bamboo thicket had the occupants of the jeep hopeful that they might witness a tiger hunting its prey. Unfortunately for them, they had no such luck.

A quarter of an hour later, the occupants of the jeep became the subjects of observation. The guide pointed to a small tree behind the jeep and softly said, 'Macaques!'

The other occupants of the vehicle turned around to find several grey monkeys looking at them curiously. A large male descended first and was followed by several other members of the troupe.

Joe saw a mother with a tiny baby clinging to her stomach and said, 'Aww, that's cute!' as he trained his camera on them and clicked away.

Finally, he lowered the camera and just enjoyed a sight that was unusual for him, but rather more common for the others. Suddenly, the large male began to walk menacingly towards the jeep. He seemed to be focused on Joe and appeared unconcerned with the rest of the men in the vehicle. When he was within ten feet of the jeep, he growled and bared his teeth.

Joe was puzzled; he wasn't sure why he was being singled out for the aggressive treatment. 'Easy, boy,' he said in a low voice.

The monkey advanced several feet further and snarled again. Joe became a bit concerned. Finally, the guide clapped his hands loudly and shouted. The large male turned around and with a last, hateful look at Joe, bounded away. The rest of the monkeys followed their leader and melted into the jungle.

'That's very unusual behaviour,' said the guide to Joe. 'Monkeys in the jungle don't normally get that close to humans. I am not sure why that male was so upset with you, sir.'

A minute later, the guide, who was a little worried about offending Joe, continued tentatively, 'Also sir, since your face is so, um, red, he may have thought you were being aggressive.'

Never at a loss for words, Chomu said, 'Oh, there's a very simple explanation. As you've all observed, since the colour of Joe's face closely matches that of a monkey's rear end, he thought Joe meant to insult him.'

When Joyappa's stomach rumbled for the third time, they decided to head back to the resort for breakfast. The naturalist chose a different route back in the hope of seeing even more wildlife. As they rounded a corner, the jeep almost hit a cow elephant and its calf, which were bang in the middle of the road. The elephants crossed the road, and the jeep stopped for a better view. The mother stood protectively by the side of the calf and faced the vehicle. Joe readied his camera and began to take pictures. Everyone else quietly enjoyed watching the animals from close range. The only sounds were of a few birds twittering in the distance, and of the guide sniffing as he periodically wiped his nose on the sleeve of his camouflage outfit.

Joe began to make a video of the elephants on his camera, when the guide began to cough. Joyappa, who was seated by the guide, wondered how such a skinny chest could produce such a horrendously loud noise. It was a deep, loud, hacking cough that took everyone by surprise. It also had the unfortunate effect of upsetting the elephants. The little one squealed in fear and the mother decided that enough was enough. Without warning, she trumpeted and charged.

Chomu, who was on the side closest to the elephants, screamed in a high pitched voice, 'Go, man! We're being attacked.' He then scooted over to the other end of the jeep and curled up in a little ball below the seat.

Joyappa had heard stories of a vehicle and its occupants being stomped to an unrecognizable mass by irate elephants. He was terrified. Later, he wondered if he had been more scared of the charging elephant or of Susheela's impending wrath.

Upon hearing Chomu's desperate call, the naturalist hit the accelerator and they sped away in a cloud of dust. Once the danger was past, although Joe felt a bit bad to have disturbed the elephants, he was secretly thrilled at the experience. He was already thinking of all the things he could tell his drinking buddies back in America about the close encounter.

Over breakfast, Joe showed everyone the photographs he had taken. He was particularly pleased with the close-ups of the elephant and its baby.

Chomu, who had evidently forgotten about his girly scream when the elephant charged, said, 'You know, Joe, if that guide hadn't panicked and driven away so fast, I bet I could have even petted that calf. I'm sure that was a mock-charge—that elephant would have stopped short of the jeep. If I'd given her a good whack on the trunk, I'm sure she would have turned and run away with her tail between her legs.'

XII

After the excitement of the safari, the men lazed about, drank too much and ate a huge lunch before setting off in a westerly direction for home. They chose to take a different route back. Joe was fascinated to observe small villages with cattle in the middle of the road, and colourful chickens foraging for food. Many of the villagers were equally fascinated with Joe's appearance and stared at him with curiosity. A stop for tender coconuts near a village quickly attracted a huge crowd that stared, and then giggled, as Joe tried to drink the coconut water without a straw and succeeded in spilling much of it on his shirt front.

Many of the back roads were in poor condition. When they reached the highway, the surface was excellent and they made good time. Chomu drove, and Joyappa tried to keep a conversation going to keep him from falling asleep after the heavy meal washed down with beer. Joe stretched out on the back seat and dozed off.

When they were about an hour from their destination, the road abruptly deteriorated. There were stones on either side indicating that plans to repair the road were afoot. However, the surface was a dusty, undulating mess which resulted in a slow, bone-jarring ride. Despite their dark glasses, Chomu and Joyappa found the late afternoon sun in their eyes added to their discomfort. Remarkably, Joe appeared to be unaffected by the rough road as he continued to snore gently in the back seat.

Chomu's car crawled along, while the sun sank lower and lower and the light began to fade. Since most travellers didn't want to risk a breakdown at night several miles from a workshop, the number of vehicles on the road dwindled until it was rare to see another car.

As they reached a densely forested area, Joyappa spotted an old red car parked by the right side of the road. The bonnet was up and a thin, bespectacled man was staring at the engine. When he saw Chomu's car, the man stepped to the edge of the road and stuck his hand out. Chomu decided to offer his assistance, as it was unlikely that anyone else would pass by so late in the day. So he pulled over to the right side and stopped in front of the battered vehicle.

Chomu and Joyappa got out and stretched their aching limbs before approaching the stranded vehicle. The motorist wore thick glasses and a diffident air. He appeared to be very relieved that someone had stopped to help.

'So, what's the problem?' said Chomu confidently.

'I'm not sure,' replied the thin man, who had a large spanner in his hand, 'but I could really use some help. Just a few minutes ago, the engine overheated. I'm not sure why.'

'Hmm,' said Chomu thoughtfully. He hadn't a clue about

what might be wrong, so he said, 'You know, it could be any number of things. Since my lower back is hurting a bit at the moment, I don't think I can bend too easily. Why don't you take a look, Joya?'

'Okay,' said Joyappa. He parked his sun glasses on his head and began to twist the radiator cap off so as to check the coolant level. It *should* have struck him that the radiator was at room temperature, when the driver of the vehicle claimed the engine had just overheated. Instead, what struck him was a blow on the back of his head from the big spanner in the motorist's hand. Fortunately for Joyappa, he had moved his head to peer at the inside of the radiator just as his assailant swung at him, so the spanner only delivered a glancing blow.

He turned around in surprise to determine what had hit him. The thin man's face was contorted into an aggressive scowl and he waved the spanner threateningly at Joyappa.

'Hey, Paunchy,' he growled, 'hand over your money. I bet you have lots of it or you wouldn't have been able to grow that huge gut.'

The insult made Joyappa very annoyed. He didn't bother to answer. Instead, he consciously tried to suck in his gut. Unfortunately, there was no noticeable difference in his waistline.

When Joyappa looked for Chomu, he saw him sitting motionless as blood dripped to the ground from a wound on his head. Now, Joyappa was furious. He looked the highwayman over and concluded that, spanner or no spanner, he was going to charge him and beat him to a pulp. As if reading his mind, the thin man let out a low whistle. Joyappa could hear some crackling in the undergrowth and two rough looking characters emerged. Both were unshaven and smelled strongly of liquor and stale sweat. They each wore tight polyester shirts over jeans decorated with multiple zippers that served no apparent purpose. The taller one carried a rusty crowbar, while his partner in crime brandished a heavy iron hammer. The new arrivals changed the odds. With Chomu incapacitated, Joyappa couldn't very well take on three armed men.

Since he seldom read anything other than the sports page of the newspaper, Joyappa was unaware that highway robbers operated in the area. Many travellers had fallen victim to the gang over the past year, so people avoided travelling through this densely forested area after dark. In the brotherhood of thieves, the leader of the gang was known as 'Spanner' Satish, and his cohorts were 'Rod' Ranga and 'Hammer' Harish.

Chomu raised his head and saw Joyappa, 'What the hell happened, Joya?' he said, with a puzzled look on his face.

Joyappa didn't answer. He was thinking of a way to get out of the situation.

The blow to Chomu's head had unfortunately caused a peculiar effect. He suddenly began to belt out the national anthem in a loud and tuneless rendition.

'Shut up!' screamed Satish, but Chomu appeared not to hear him. Instead, he shakily got to his feet, stood at attention, and continued to sing.

Satish was getting upset, but realized that any discussion with Chomu in his present state would be pointless, so he turned his attention to Joyappa, again. 'Come on. Hand over your money,' he growled.

Joyappa ignored him. He was still thinking.

Satish waved his spanner in front of Joyappa's face and said, 'Give me the money or I'll whack you again.'

'You won't get away with this. If you're so tough why don't you fight one on one like a man?'

'Shut up!' screamed Satish, 'If you don't give us your money—we're going to beat you up and take it from you.'

'I don't *have* much money,' said Joyappa, 'I just spent most of it.'

The leader signaled to Harish, who brandished his hammer as he approached Joyappa, and ordered him to raise his hands. Joyappa reluctantly complied with the order.

'Aha!' said Harish triumphantly when he noticed the bulge in Joyappa's back pocket caused by his wallet.

Harish transferred the hammer to his left hand and tried to remove the wallet. However, Joyappa's jeans were much too tight; Harish tugged hard but the wallet wouldn't budge. Harish never practised the art of picking pockets as he considered his own violent vocation superior. His lack of success was understandable, as even a seasoned 'pickpocket' might have found the task challenging. Satish was getting impatient, so Harish dropped the hammer in frustration and yanked at the wallet with both hands.

At this point, Chomu had reached the middle of the national anthem and grown confused about the next verse (which he never really understood anyway). Still standing ramrod straight, Chomu suddenly began to sing something that sounded like 'Ba Ba Black Sheep'.

The sudden and unexpected change in musical genres caused the crooks to pause and stare at Chomu. Harish was so surprised that he actually sat down. Sensing his opportunity, Joyappa quickly brought his elbow down towards Harish's face. The elbow made contact with Harish's nose with a satisfying (to Joyappa) *crunch*. Harish squealed and grabbed his broken nose. Joyappa quickly picked up the hammer and faced Ranga and Satish.

Ranga and his leader were quite surprised as they normally didn't encounter any resistance during their hold-ups. They glanced at Harish, who was on his haunches nursing his broken nose, as a mixture of blood and other fluids ran down his face. Neither of them seemed particularly sympathetic to his plight, and they quickly turned their attention back to Joyappa.

They approached Joyappa threateningly, but with some caution, as he was now armed with Harish's weapon.

At this point, Joe finally woke up and was surprised to find himself alone in the stationary vehicle. So he rubbed his eyes and looked out, only to be met with a very strange scene.

For some reason, Chomu was standing at attention with his hand over his heart. His hair was matted with blood as he sang about a black sheep. Abruptly, Chomu switched tunes, and began to sing even louder about Mary and her white lamb. Joyappa was crouched defensively as he waved a large hammer before him. Two rough looking men armed with a crowbar and spanner, respectively, walked menacingly towards Joyappa. Another stranger was clutching his nose as he squatted by Joyappa's side.

It was clear to Joe that his friends were in trouble. Normally, Joe was a peace-loving, easy going sort of fellow. However, on the football field, his opponents were well aware that Joe Scurlock was transformed to a borderline crazy person. Joe himself had lost count of the number of rivals he had caused to be 'stretchered' off the field with concussions, sprains, broken bones and bruises, during his college career. Upon seeing

Joyappa being attacked, Joe's personality underwent a dramatic change. Now, he had his game face on.

Joe carefully opened the door of the car and approached Joyappa's assailants from behind. Since Chomu was loudly and tunelessly belting out pastoral tunes, there was no danger of anyone hearing Joe's footsteps. Ranga took a swing at Joyappa's head with his crowbar. Joyappa managed to duck and avoid harm. Joe quickly assessed the situation, and decided that the man swinging the crowbar would be his first target. So he started a lumbering charge towards him and built up a good head of steam. As Ranga lifted his crowbar again, Joe's right shoulder made violent contact with the robber's back. Joe knew that the leverage, timing and power of the hit were perfect, and his old college coach would have been proud. The crowbar fell harmlessly to the ground, a couple of Ranga's ribs cracked, and he was lifted cleanly off his feet before crashing head-first against a nearby tree. Joe savoured the collision, which gave him just as much satisfaction as knocking out a quarterback during a football game.

Satish looked around in shock. That was all Joyappa needed, and he brought the hammer down on Satish's huge spanner, which went flying away into the brush. As Satish made a move to retrieve his weapon, Joyappa grabbed him by the neck and shook him so violently that the thick glasses fell off his face revealing a pair of bulging, myopic eyes.

Satish was dazed. In all his attempts at highway robbery, this sort of thing had never occurred. He realized that he alone had to contend with three men, one of whom was the biggest human being he had had the misfortune to encounter.

Looking at Joe's angry red face and frothing mouth, and

Joyappa's stern visage, Satish's attitude underwent a sea change. He smiled, revealing red, betel-stained teeth and obsequiously said, 'Sir, sir, it was just a big mistake. I was just joking with you.'

'Joking, huh? We'll see about that in a minute,' said Joyappa.

As Joe stood guard, Joyappa went to the car, got some water and splashed it on Chomu's face. Chomu finally stopped singing. Joyappa then disinfected Chomu's head wound using the first aid kit from his car.

After Chomu drank some water, he seemed to regain his wits. He rubbed his temples and asked, 'What happened, Joya?'

Joyappa explained the situation to Chomu. Meanwhile, the leader of the dacoits had put on his glasses and was doing his best to ingratiate himself with Joe, who still had his game face on and was raring to tackle someone else.

'Sir, you are English? Oh, I love English people. In India, we hosted English people for hundreds of years. My first name is English. Sir, what is *your* good name?'

Joe didn't know how to react to Satish's pleasant chitchat— so he now sported a somewhat puzzled game face.

'Shut up! We'll do the questioning,' said Joyappa before Joe could respond.

Joyappa dragged Harish and the now semi-conscious Ranga over to where Satish was seated.

By now, Chomu was feeling much better. He swaggered over to join his friends. Since he was still a bit unsteady on his feet, the swagger looked all the more threatening to the thugs.

Chomu was now in his element. His normally protuberant lower jaw jutted even further forward. His normally red eyes were even redder than before. Chomu then proceeded, with great eloquence, to describe to his captive audience what he planned to do to them. The speech was embellished with actions that would have done a seasoned thespian proud.

Satish's glasses were soon covered with a thin film of saliva as Chomu described in excruciating detail how he would extract his pound of flesh from the thugs. In keeping with the gang's theme, Chomu threw in references to needle-nose pliers, wire cutters, ball peen hammers, screw drivers, hacksaws, chain saws, chisels and other such assorted tools. Satish turned pale and didn't even bother to wipe his glasses clean. Instead, he threw up all over Harish's sandal-clad feet. Harish began to cry, adding yet another fluid to the mess running down his face. Ranga, still stunned from the monster hit he had received, started shivering before slipping back into unconsciousness.

In fact, Chomu's monologue and actions were *so* graphic that Joyappa couldn't take it anymore. He wandered off and pretended to make a call on his cell phone. Even Joe, who caught the gist of the speech, was so horrified that he feigned being thirsty, went back to the car and drank some water.

Finally, Chomu paused. His head had begun to hurt again and his throat felt a bit parched. He decided that he could do with the beer he'd stashed away in his vehicle. So he strutted over to the car and rummaged around the cooler until he found a can. He took a swig and swaggered back to where he'd left the three highwaymen to tell them what *exactly* he would do with a power drill. However, he was astonished to find that the three men had suddenly vanished!

The gang's departure must have been a hurried one, since they'd left not only the tools of their trade, but also Satish's glasses and (understandably) Harish's soiled sandals.

Chomu could actually hear the men crashing through the undergrowth, but decided not to pursue them. Instead, Joyappa and Chomu 'took care' of the gang's little red car. The two men, with the help of the hammer and crowbar, smashed the car's engine and deflated its tyres to ensure that the dacoits wouldn't be able to go far. They figured that it would be a long, hard walk to the nearest town through thick jungle rife with elephants and big cats.

Joyappa hoped that the abortive bid at highway robbery and the subsequent punishment would serve as a deterrent to the gang. He resolved to provide a censored version of the events of the evening to law enforcement.

When they resumed their journey, Joyappa went on about how Joe's charge had saved them from robbery and possibly worse. In great detail, Joyappa described the power behind the tackle and its effect on Ranga. Chomu was impressed, and never questioned or put down the toughness of American football players, again. The rehashing of the attempted hold-up reminded the former ball players of the bonding between teammates after a game and suffused them with a warm, satisfied glow.

As Chomu drove up Joyappa's driveway, he noticed that Susheela's car was back, so he parted sadly from his friends and drove back home quickly. Susheela must have just returned, as the engine of her car was still hot. Joyappa hoped that she hadn't seen his car parked in the garage, or noticed Chomu dropping them back home.

When they entered the house, Susheela greeted Joe and Joyappa warmly. Her mother had recovered well, but she still felt bad that she had abandoned their guest during his visit.

'So how was the trip, Joe?'

'It was great, Sue. I really enjoyed myself.'

'That's good,' said Susheela, 'I hope you had a quiet, relaxing time. I was worried you would get into trouble with Joy.'

'No, no. We had no trouble,' interjected Joyappa, quickly.

'It *was* a relaxing time, Sue,' said Joe, and Joyappa breathed a sigh of relief.

XIII

A couple of days later, it was time for Joe to go back to America. Susheela decided to accompany Joyappa when he drove Joe to the airport. Since Susheela was with them, Joyappa did not make any unscheduled stops or detours for questionable purposes. The journey was uneventful and they got Joe to the airport on time.

After giving each of his hosts a bear hug, Joe said, 'This has been a fantastic vacation, guys. I just can't thank you enough. I've got some great memories. Heck, if I didn't have to get back to work, I'd have loved to stay longer.' He meant every word.

Susheela had a moment of doubt as to whether Joyappa had got their guest involved in undesirable activities. *I guess I'll find out soon enough*, she thought.

'Have a safe trip, Joe, and give my love to Patty. I hope both of you can visit us next time.'

'Thanks, Sue,' he said, thinking that there was no way he would have had as much fun with Joyappa and Chomu if Patty had accompanied him. 'Say, you guys must visit us. We'd love to have you over.'

'Thanks, bro',' said Joyappa, sadly, 'maybe we will get

there someday.' He wished Joe could have stayed with them permanently.

'Have a safe journey, Joe. Make sure all your travel documents are handy, and in order,' said Susheela.

'Not to worry, guys. I've got my passport and ticket on me.'

As Joe entered the departure lounge, he waved. Joyappa and Susheela waved back. While Joe wheeled his luggage towards the airline counter, his attention was diverted to a little coffee shop. In the display case, Joe spotted a tray of chocolate doughnuts—the sight of which made his stomach rumble. Joe looked around, but could not see his hosts outside the departure lounge. Since the desire for his comfort food was overpowering, and as he believed that even if Susheela was still outside she wouldn't be able to spot him amongst all the other travellers, Joe decided to indulge his sweet tooth. Outside the airport, Joyappa was off looking for a rest room, but Susheela was watching carefully to make sure that Joe's check-in went smoothly.

Susheela saw the large red-headed figure look around like a jackal about to launch a raid on a hen house, before approaching the pretty girl in the coffee shop. As he was placing his order, Joe paused, open-mouthed, to observe an attractive woman walk past in high heels.

'*That snake!*' muttered Susheela, while she saw him purchasing a whole bag of doughnuts.

Joe was in the process of walking towards the airline counter when he felt the urge to scratch himself in a place where one normally wouldn't scratch in public. In his defense, the leech bites he had suffered during the trek continued to be a source of irritation. As Joe happily, and quite unselfconsciously, surrendered to his urge, Susheela blinked in horrified disapproval.

Joe's exertions had the unfortunate consequence of dislodging his passport from his hip pocket. Susheela watched helplessly as the passport fell on the floor–seemingly in slow motion. She screamed Joe's name. Joe couldn't hear her, but as he stood in queue, he quickly disposed of two doughnuts with a pleased look on his face. As he got closer to the airline counter, Joe dusted crumbs from his chin and began to fumble in his pockets for his travel documents. He pulled out the air ticket, but couldn't locate his passport. His heart missed a beat and he turned pale as he looked around frantically. Fortunately for Joe, Susheela had alerted airport security, and a uniformed employee had already picked up the passport.

'Are you looking for this, sir?' asked the security man.

'Thank God!' said Joe with relief. Then he grabbed the passport, thanked the airport employee and shook his hand so vigourously that the poor man was in danger of dislocating a shoulder.

Later, as Joyappa drove to a hotel in the city, Susheela said, 'Thanks a lot, Joy, for taking care of Joe when I was away.'

'It was no problem, Susheela. He was easy to entertain and I quite enjoyed his visit. I just wish we could have kept him.' said Joyappa, a bit sadly.

Then, he remembered Joe's invitation and resolved to work especially hard, harvest a bumper crop and save enough money for a vacation. Joyappa cheered up as he thought of how much fun he could have in America with his new pal. If he played his cards right, and waited until Susheela had some unavoidable commitment with her women's self-help group, he could make the trip with just Chomu and Charlie, instead.

In the meanwhile, Susheela kept thinking that Joe reminded

her of someone, but she couldn't decide just who it was. Finally, as they checked into their hotel, she was suddenly struck by a thought and whispered to herself, '*Oh...My...God!* Patty and I have more in common than I thought. *Joe is the American version of Joy!*'

Author's Note

Hopefully, Joyappa and his friends have elicited some laughs during the course of their adventures. Now that Joyappa has found that he gets along famously with his American guest, his thoughts are very much on a visit to the USA.

I am certain that there will be rampant speculation as to whether the characters featured in this book represent real-life individuals. I would like to emphasize, for the record (as well as for my own well-being), that this is a work of fiction.

On a more serious note, perhaps the description of the animals, plants and geography of Coorg (Kodagu) will encourage young people with roots in this picturesque little district to retain their properties or even acquire land in this area. In the name of development, the destruction of wetlands, forests and plantations will not only have an adverse ecological impact on Coorg, but will also severely affect the livelihood of millions of people who depend on the streams and rivers that originate here. So, despite the often harsh conditions, poor infrastructure and the uncertainties of agriculture, I hope that both the present and future residents of this area will be vigilant about protecting the environment of Coorg from undesirable change.

I thank Coffeeland News and Kodagu Connect for previously publishing, under a nom de plume, a couple of chapters that feature in this book.

I am very grateful to Patricia Taylor for her encouragement and many useful suggestions. I am also appreciative of the fact that she inadvertently proved to be a bright (red) inspiration for one of the stories, after being exposed to the harsh tropical sun during a trek.

Glossary

Ajja or *Thatha*	Grandfather
Akki otti	Flat bread made from rice and rice flour
Avvaya	Grandmother
Chakkuli	Fried snack, typically slightly salty
Dammayya	Please
Kesari bath	Sweet dish, flavoured with saffron
Koile meen	Very small, edible fish found in streams
Kolé puttu	Sweet dish made from either bananas or jackfruit, wrapped in a banana leaf and steamed before serving
Molay	Daughter (term of endearment)
Monay	Son (term of endearment)
Naati ota	Race conducted in wet, slushy paddy fields
Pandi curry	Rich, dark pork curry supplemented with local ingredients
Telomere	DNA found at the ends of our chromosomes; thought to be protective in function. Shortening of telomeres is believed to be associated with aging
Ubba	Gate made from bamboo poles